Model Railroading with M.T.H. Electric Trains

Rob Adelman

Photography by Carlos Navarrete

Design and compilation ©2002 by Krause Publications, Inc.

M.T.H. photographic train images and all related M.T.H. Electric Trains logos ©2002 by M.T.H. Electric Trains®, used with permission.

Published by

krause publications
700 East State Street • Iola, WI 54990-0001

Please call or write for our free catalog of publications. To place an order or obtain a free catalog, please call (800) 258-0929. Please use our regular business telephone (715) 445-2214 for editorial comment or further information.

Library of Congress Catalog Number 2002105775
ISBN 0-87349-350-8

Dedication

I would like to dedicate this book to my Dad. *The time you spent playing trains with me on our living room floor as I grew up was absolutely priceless.*

Acknowledgments

I would like to take a few moments to convey my deep appreciation to those who helped in the process of writing this book. It was a long and arduous road, but there is no doubt in my mind that, without the participation of the following people and companies, this book would have never made it to print.

First, I would like to thank Mike Wolf, president and chief executive officer of M.T.H. Electric Trains. Mike, without your vision and willingness to take bold and innovative risks, the O Gauge segment of model railroading would never have experienced the renaissance in the marketplace that it has over the last eight years. Thank you, Andy Edleman and Kristin Bailey of M.T.H. Electric Trains, for your time and willingness to help with the items I needed for the Santa Fe Raton Pass Railroad, and also for answering questions I had throughout the entire process of writing the book. Thank you to Ruean Holt and the good folks at Woodland Scenics for providing your products for the train layout. Thank you to BackDrop Warehouse for your willingness to take part in this book. Many heartfelt thanks to Allan Miller; you not only helped this book project get going, but you contributed greatly by giving your advice and direction regarding the writing, as well as helping me with the text. Thank you also to the TOOGs: Clktyclack, Gazaer, HIBBY-GIBI, HOLIT, Hydra5, Jscu870705, MacCam98, MAdams4228, OGColl, O Trains, Razz702, RTTAZ54, Shrugger59, SSW4ME, SteveJMJr, and TAG 18. I appreciate the help and input from each of you, along with your friendship. We have all built a strong bond through our interaction via AOL and the Internet, and the deep knowledge of, and dedication to, the hobby by each of you is an inspiration to me. A great big thank you to my wonderful father-in-law, Ted Cheatham; thank you, Ted, for your immense help and advice in constructing the Santa Fe Raton Pass Railroad for the book. And thank you to Kenny Barnes, Bob Hill, Jim Jenkens, Cheryl McClain, Dan Pitcock, and Frank Wilkins. I would also like to thank my dad; if you hadn't introduced me to toy trains at the age of five, I may never have experienced this wonderful hobby. I additionally must give enormous thanks to my lovely wife, Amie, and daughter, Elizabeth; thank you so much for your patience, support, and many times sacrificial giving towards the completion of this book. Last, but certainly not least, I would like to thank my Lord and Savior Jesus Christ; for it is only through You that all things are possible – including this book.

Table of Contents

Foreword

After more than 100 years of action, model railroading may well have entered its greatest era in the 21st century. A hobby long steeped in tradition continues to carry forth its basic appeal of miniaturization, movement and action. Unlike the second half of its first century, however, model railroading's entry in the new millennium is infused with products featuring state-of-the-art technology designed to lift the hobby from the gloom of a basement to the brightness of a family room.

Fueled by phenomenal growth spurred on primarily by baby-boom-generation men, model railroading now has a chance to appeal to an entirely new generation of consumers, thanks to incredible advances in technology and product choices. With virtually every gauge supported by a half a dozen or more manufacturers, modelers can find miniatures of almost every train, railcar, building, track configuration, and trackside component that ever existed in real life. In the O gauge marketplace, product choice has outpaced all other gauges in the past decade. During this "revolution," M.T.H. Electric Trains has proudly led all manufacturers in product expansion through the promotion of over 5,200 different M.T.H. items since 1992.

Technology has played an even more important role than greater product choices in the growth of O gauge model railroading. For the most part, model railroading relied on the same technology as that found in toy train products manufactured in the 1940s and '50s. By the early 1990s, digital sound was heard in M.T.H. products. Heralded for their sound quality, these sound-equipped locomotives began to awaken model railroading enthusiasts to the potential of owning a realistic looking and operating model railroad. While praised for their quality and realism, these early "digital" trains still lacked one primary feature needed to make each a unique element on the layout.

The single greatest development in model railroading has been the transition from fixed or conventional control to "command control," where each element of the model railroad layout can be independently operated – even multiple engines on the same track at the same time! Historically, control over toy train locomotives had been accomplished in the same manner as that used in the early 20th century. A power supply or transformer energized the rails of the track, which caused all engines to move at speeds governed by the amount of current on the rails. Independent control over each locomotive – like that in real life – was not easily obtainable. A command control system elevates model railroading to an almost 3D digital video game, in which operators independ-ently select elements of the layout (locomotives, accessories, track switches, and more), and operate them through a wireless, remote control. With the release of M.T.H.'s Digital Command System or DCS, this concept has been elevated even further thanks to incredible advances made possible through the inclusion of the latest wireless technology. Hundreds of features are included in DCS that allow operators almost unimaginable control of their layout from just a few years ago.

More important than the features found in a command control system like DCS is the appeal such control will have to younger consumers – those children and grandchildren of the baby boomers who have long supported the model railroading tradition. For the first time in more than fifty years, model railroading has a chance to say to a new enthusiast, "Hey, this is a cool hobby." With hundreds of programmable options, future computer interface control, and the ability to customize the model railroad to the operator's individual tastes, DCS favorably compares to today's more well-known consumer electronic play toys – video and pc games. Yet, it provides more wholesomeness, educational value, and practical skill lessons than any video or pc game could hope to offer.

Today's families are looking for ways to participate in activities together. Model railroading long ago provided that outlet, but had lost the ability to capture a younger audience inundated with literally thousands of choices in a $100-billion toy market. While model railroading doesn't have the marketing clout behind it to recapture the large market share it controlled in the 1950s, it does have the ability to stand out as an innovative, educational, and exciting alternative for today's families looking for pastimes they can participate in together.

The combination of technology, modeling, realism, and miniaturization has historically best been exemplified through model railroading. Building easy-to-use track systems, like M.T.H.'s RealTrax, high-quality ready-to-run train sets like those found in the M.T.H. RailKing line, and the incredible realism of the DCS command control system is what separates M.T.H. from other model railroad manufacturers. For M.T.H. Electric Trains, creating those elements gives families a chance to dive into a hobby that could bind them together for generations. Witnessing those occurrences always reminds us of the importance of our mission.

-Mike Wolf

CHAPTER 1

Introduction

A RailKing Santa Fe E-3 diesel engine heading up the Super Chief *rumbles into Raton passing by the Rio Grande Avenue crossing.*

Imposing and powerful, the locomotive rumbles past you on its way into the train station. Trailing behind is a string of passenger cars, resplendent in their stainless steel finish. The throbbing roar of diesel engines is suddenly punctuated by a higher-pitched whine as the train's engineer eases back on the throttle, reducing the power. Brakes squeal in protest as they bring the harnessed, gleaming beast gradually and gracefully to a halt. An air of anticipation hangs over those who have been patiently waiting on the station platform. *"Now arriving from Chicago, Train #17, the Santa Fe Super Chief,"* the loudspeaker blares.

Within moments, passenger car doors open with a "clank," and a train crewman steps down to assist passengers exiting the train. *"Watch your step,"* he cautions.

The previously quiet station platform becomes a wildly animated scene, with passengers scurrying about and baggage handlers, train crew, and other railroad employees carrying out their duties with equal vigor. *"Baggage to your right!"* shouts a redcap. *"Thank you sir! Have a nice day!"* is the oft-repeated message from the conductor as he bids goodbye to his former charges. *"Hold that taxi!"* shouts a travel-weary passenger in a hurry to get home.

You watch this action unfold, and you are reminded of a time in our nation's history when such scenes were commonplace – a part of everyday life for millions of travelers. But today, in the early years of a new century, such scenarios are rare … unless, of course, you are enjoying this action in miniature on a model railroad created with M.T.H. Electric Trains!

The truth is, virtually every detail described above – from the arrival of the rumbling locomotive to the interplay of voices along the station platform – is just a part of the many sights and sounds that can be seen and heard regularly on M.T.H. model railroads throughout the country. It's all part of a new era in O gauge model railroading; an era ushered in by a young and energetic entrepreneur named Mike Wolf, who was determined from the start to offer products that

A RailKing Santa Fe Hudson steam engine passes by the water tower at Starkville.

the world of model railroading with M.T.H. trains.

M.T.H. Electric Trains, under the leadership of founder Mike Wolf, sparked a rejuvenation of interest in O gauge model railroading that quickly blazed into a full-blown revolution. Since the mid-1990s, M.T.H. has introduced more new products and more new product features to the hobby than had been seen at any previous point in O gauge railroading's long history. It can truthfully be said that M.T.H. Electric Trains created what amounts to a whole new era of O gauge model railroading by maintaining the quality and tradition of yesterday's electric trains, while advancing the hobby to a higher level via an ever-expanding variety of innovative items with increased realism and true-to-prototype operational capabilities. It's little wonder that, in less than a decade, M.T.H. products have become the most talked about and sought-after items in the hobby.

Simply owning M.T.H. Electric Trains is not enough, even for most of those who are inclined to collect, display, and admire these colorful models. To fully enjoy the many features of these superb examples of railroading in miniature, the hobbyist also needs to operate the trains and accessories. That is what this book – the first comprehensive manual designed to cover the full spectrum of planning, building, and operating a model railroad with M.T.H. Electric Trains – is all about.

Of course, those new to the hobby might reasonably ask: "Why model railroading?" or, "Why O gauge," or even "Why model railroading with M.T.H. Electric Trains?" – all perfectly logical questions posed by someone just getting started. So, let's spend a bit of time addressing each in turn.

blended realism with state-of-the-art technology, while still maintaining the quality and tradition of the famed toy trains of yesteryear.

So, I now bid you welcome to the fascinating world of realistic model railroading with M.T.H. Electric Trains! If you've been involved in the model railroading hobby for a time, you likely have heard about M.T.H. Electric Trains, and you may already own some of the products produced by them. If you're new to the hobby, or just considering a new activity for your leisure hours, you truly do owe it to yourself to explore

Why Model Railroading?

Simply put, there probably is no more infinitely varied and creative hobby around! I'm a bit biased about this, of course, but I'm also hard-pressed to think of any hobby that can be so fully shared with family and friends, or one that encompasses so much: Historical research, carpentry, electronics and electrical work, model building, artistry, mechanics, and a host of other areas. You don't need to be an expert in any of these areas, because you'll master the fundamentals of each as you learn and progress in an easy-to-do fashion. It's a hobby that can be as simple or complex as you want it to be, and it is tailored for virtually every budget. Best of all, perhaps, model railroading is a great "stress-reduction" activity. In fact, it is

The switch tower at Trinidad with the majestic Rocky Mountains in the background.

It is nighttime as passengers wait for El Capitan *passenger train at the Raton station.*

recommended by many physicians and psychologists as an ideal way to manage stress.

Why O Gauge?

O gauge trains, which are 1/48 the size of their real-life prototypes if they are made to exact scale, are just about the ideal size for handling and operating. M.T.H. Electric Trains currently offers electric trains in three scales or gauges: O gauge, Standard Gauge, and #1 gauge. O gauge comprises, by far, their largest and most varied line, and enjoys the greatest following. Standard Gauge trains are replicas of the larger-than-O-gauge electric trains that were popular in the early decades of the twentieth century. These are true "tin-plate" trains, meaning that they are primarily made of metal, and are fanciful re-creations loosely based on real prototypes. The new M.T.H. #1 gauge trains are also larger than O gauge, and are made to a 1/32 scale that is often preferred by those who are involved in a segment of the hobby known as "garden rail-roading"; these trains actually operate outdoors. In general, though, O gauge trains are just about ideally sized for small and large hands, for easy use by young and old alike, and they are rugged, durable, and sized right for a full-fledged operating layout in most

homes. In short, they are right for most model rail-roading applications and for model railroad enthusiasts of any age.

Why Model Railroading with M.T.H. Electric Trains?

M.T.H. trains offer more variety, value, and features for the dollar than any competing brand. In the entire history of the hobby, no firm has produced such an astounding variety of trains, track, and accessories for O gauge railroaders in such a relatively short time. And, there's something in the M.T.H. line for every budget, from the affordable RailKing and Rugged Rails lines to the highly detailed Premier offerings. Generally, all RailKing and Rugged Rails items are made to approximately 1/48 scale, and they can be operated on any O gauge railroad. Most Premier items, which are made to true 1/48 scale, may be significantly larger or longer, depending on their prototype's actual dimensions, and these items may require larger-radius curves for proper operation. The point is, there is something for every interest in the M.T.H. range, and no other manufacturer offers such an extensive variety.

You can, of course, operate and enjoy your M.T.H. Electric Trains along with other brands of O gauge

With heavy smoke, the RailKing Santa Fe Hudson emerges from the tunnel on Raton Pass.

Who says you cannot have a lot of action in a small space? Several industries provide for plenty of switching opportunities in the town of Trinidad.

trains and accessories that are made for three-rail O gauge operations. But with the variety of items already available – and more on the way all the time – who really needs to look elsewhere?

In these pages, you'll learn all about the history of M.T.H. and see the special features that distinguish M.T.H. Electric Trains from all others. M.T.H. trains are the most realistic appearing, sounding, and performing trains available in any scale.

You'll learn about the simplicity and versatility of the M.T.H. track system, and see why it is the ideal way to keep trains running smoothly and reliably, whether on the floor around the Christmas tree or on a permanent model railroad layout.

You'll also learn about the various options that are available for powering your trains, ranging from conventional transformer control to the state-of-the-art DCS command control system that truly affords you as much, or more, control than that available to real locomotive engineers.

Perhaps most importantly, you'll learn how to plan, construct, wire, control, and detail a complete model railroad designed to fit a small space that will provide endless hours of creative enjoyment. If you follow the step-by-step instructions, the result will be a functional and attractive layout that you will be proud to share with family and friends. You'll even learn to operate your railroad in a realistic manner through the "Dispatcher Game."

Here, you'll find just about all the information you need to fully participate in a hobby that will keep your interest and spark your imagination for a lifetime. Even if you're an experienced hobbyist, you'll find some new tips and techniques that can enhance your model railroading.

Model railroading is truly a fascinating and wonderful hobby. So, whether you are just getting started or are already a seasoned veteran, you'll find this book both beneficial and enlightening in a variety of ways. I will be your guide on this journey through the wonderful world of model railroading with M.T.H. Electric Trains, and I sincerely hope that you will enjoy the trip. It's great to have you aboard!

Rob Adelman

CHAPTER 2

History of M.T.H. Electric Trains

Mike Wolf, Founder and President of M.T.H. Electric Trains in the train room at M.T.H.'s Headquarters in Columbia, MD.

In the last several years, M.T.H. Electric Trains has experienced a meteoric rise in the O gauge market. Never before has a company made such a large and lasting impact on the hobby. An excellent illustration of this tremendous growth is found when comparing the first M.T.H. catalog in 1993 to today's catalogs: Only 15 separate items were promoted in the 1993 edition, while in 2002, a mere nine years later, three separate catalogs promoted a grand total of 1,466 items. And more products continue to keep coming from M.T.H., giving the O gauge enthusiast incredible choices never before experienced in the hobby. This astounding ascent didn't happen by coincidence, but rather through the hard work and determination of its founder, Mike Wolf, and the employees of M.T.H. Electric Trains.

Williams Reproductions

It all started back in February of 1973. Then, when Mike Wolf was just 12 years old, he began working for Williams Reproductions Limited. Jerry Williams lived in Mike's neighborhood in Howard County, Maryland, and employed Mike and his schoolmates to assemble reproductions of tinplate trains already on the market. Mike spent almost every Saturday in Williams' basement performing the intricate work of assembling latch couplers for reproductions of prewar Lionel trains. Jerry Williams paid Mike and his friends well and they enjoyed the work. Mike continued to work for Williams throughout his high school and college years. But by July 1980, Mike started his own small business venture: Mike's Train House.

A House Full of Trains

When Mike's Train House was born, Mike was working full-time as "second in command" at Williams Reproductions, and Mike's Train House was really a sideline business. The name *Mike's Train House* was truly the perfect description of what his parent's home had become, as Mike ran his sideline operation of selling William's trains directly out of his home. This meant that all the merchandise was also stored there. It was a wonder that Mike could find his

The home of Mike's parents where M.T.H. first began.

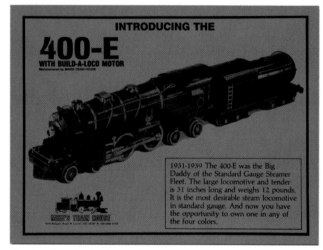

INTRODUCING THE

400-E
WITH BUILD-A-LOCO MOTOR
Manufactured by MIKES TRAIN HOUSE

1931-1939 The 400-E was the Big Daddy of the Standard Gauge Steamer Fleet. The large locomotive and tender is 31 inches long and weighs 12 pounds. It is the most desirable steam locomotive in standard gauge. And now you have the opportunity to own one in any of the four colors.

MIKE'S TRAIN HOUSE

The brochure for the Prewar Tinplate reproduction of the 400E

Mike Wolf and Se Yong Lee of Samhongsa, Ltd.

bed at night – his second floor bedroom had become a train warehouse!

It wasn't too long before Mike's Train House became one of the biggest and most successful dealers for Williams Reproductions. Naturally, Mike had plans to grow Mike's Train House, and when Williams was ready to sell his parts business in 1982, Mike jumped at the chance to buy it. Mike purchased the inventory and rights to use Williams' tooling and dies. By 1983, Jerry Williams was looking to get out of the standard gauge business altogether. He wanted to sell all his standard gauge tooling, which included all the stamping dies and tools accumulated from 1970 through 1983. Mike immediately realized this was a fantastic opportunity and was able to purchase them. Then, Mike's Train House was actually in the business of manufacturing model trains.

Giving Customers What They Want

Ever mindful of customers and the toy train products they sought, Mike purchased a black Lionel 400E locomotive with brass trim for $1,500. Many hobbyists couldn't afford the 400E at $1,500, nor could they consider running it since operating such engines decreases their value, and Mike knew it. He planned to reproduce it with the exact detail as the original, at a much lower price to the public, and with the added benefit that it could be operated because it was a reproduction. Since the engine would be die-cast, Mike invested in the tooling equipment to make it. The 400E turned out to be a big success. It continued to raise the bar of the business, and it also became part of the M.T.H. logo used throughout the late 1990s.

Relationship with Samhongsa

In 1985, the first venture between Mike and Samhongsa, a Korean manufacturer, was reproduction rolling stock of the Lionel 200 series freight cars. Once Mike received the cars from Samhongsa, he knew this was the beginning of a great relationship, as the cars were of high quality and were manufactured at an agreeable price. Mike knew they would easily sell to hobbyists. Since that time, the relationship between M.T.H. and Samhongsa has remained extremely strong, characterized by great loyalty to one another.

Busting at the Seams!

When Mike was 25 years old, he made the decision to pursue his own interests with undivided commitment. He left Williams' employ and, though he still sold Williams products, he focused more intensely on selling his own model railroading products.

The first ever die-cast Challenger Steam Engine in O gauge.

With Mike's increased business activity, he also needed increased working space. M.T.H. was rapidly expanding by now, evidenced by the acquisition of ten units in a new office complex at 9693 Gerwig Lane, Columbia, Maryland. The move to Gerwig Lane also marked the beginning of the "Thursday Night Club," a regularly occurring "open house" including train collectors, some non-train collectors, and occasional guest speakers.

Chugging Along with the Big Boys, Growing into a Major Player

From 1969 to 1989, General Mills, MPC Fundimensions and Kenner Parker manufactured Lionel products which allowed companies like M.T.H. to make reproductions of earlier Lionel products without much trouble. The only stipulation they had was that the Lionel name could not be included on the item. That changed in 1986 when Richard Kughn purchased Lionel. Though Kughn began to assert legal pressure on other companies that were making Lionel reproductions and related parts, for some reason Mike's Train House was never threatened with any formal legal action. And quite frankly, M.T.H. really wasn't concerned about it. Legal counsel held the opinion that if any action were taken against M.T.H. that the case would not stand since any copyrights on the trains M.T.H. was producing were outdated and Lionel wasn't producing any of the same trains that M.T.H. was.

In October 1986, Lionel contacted Samhongsa to propose they build model trains for Lionel. Lionel knew of the success that M.T.H. was enjoying in the market because of the high quality products that Samhongsa was making for them. However, Samhongsa, being intensely loyal to M.T.H, declined Lionel's proposal. Mike Wolf, seeing the business opportunity in this situation contacted Lionel and proposed a business relationship involving M.T.H.,

Samhongsa and Lionel. Lionel refused Mike's offer, but turned around again in early 1987 and tried to make another deal with Samhongsa which was also rejected.

By July 1987, the unexpected happened. Mike received a call from Lionel asking if they could meet together in person in a month and discuss how they might work together. To prepare for the meeting, Mike and his attorney worked to develop a contract. In brief, the contract would have M.T.H. step out of the tinplate market for five years and produce tinplate trains under the Lionel name, guarantee M.T.H. minimum purchasing amounts of the tinplate trains from Lionel, and M.T.H. would maintain the parts business and change the name to the Lionel Classic Service Center. In addition, Mike purchased an original Lionel O gauge Hiawatha set, had Samhongsa quote him a price for producing the set (after agreeing to the possible three-party arrangement), and developed a formal proposal for production of the Hiawatha under the Lionel name that would be presented along with the contract.

Once it was time for the meeting with Lionel,

The notorious MTH Dash-8 Brochure that led to the dissolving of the relationship between Mike Wolf and Lionel which helped to propel M.T.H. Electric Trains to prominence in the O gauge market today.

Mike was ready to get down to business. Lionel started off the meeting by stating that they felt Mike was in violation of their trademark by making reproductions and that they would be willing to come to some possible arrangement with M.T.H. Mike handed them a copy of the draft of the contract he had prepared, as well as the quote for producing the Hiawatha set. Lionel was taken a bit off guard as they were surprised that Mike had taken the time to have all those documents prepared. They admitted that it was too much for them to absorb right then and they needed more time. Three months later Lionel and M.T.H. had a contract with one another that would guarantee Mike income for five years. He informed all of his valued customers of the new relationship with Lionel and very quickly Mike became one of Lionel's biggest dealers.

Major Derailment, Fresh Start

Disagreements between Mike and Lionel began to occur. A newly renegotiated contract eliminated the minimum purchase provision M.T.H. had previously enjoyed. Following disagreements over the manufacturing, the relationship between M.T.H. and Lionel was officially dissolved and Lionel terminated M.T.H.'s dealership contract.

But opportunity beckoned. With the curtain finally closed on his relationship with Lionel, Mike was now free to pursue his vision like never before, and M.T.H. hit the ground running.

Mike's vision for model railroading was soon to lead M.T.H. to produce more locomotives and new product lines than any other company had in many years prior. His first project was to produce a die-cast scale model of the Union Pacific Challenger – the first ever die-cast articulated engine produced for O gauge.

The Challenger was the beginning of M.T.H.'s Premier Line of steam locomotives and, when it was announced, only a few orders came in, as hobbyists were unsure what it would be like. However, once production models became available, hobbyists saw that the Challenger was of such high quality that the orders just came pouring in. M.T.H. had hit a home run. They proved their design ability, production expertise, and their capacity to produce the engines.

Once M.T.H. began manufacturing under the M.T.H. logo, they stopped selling other lines of model train items. As a result, their dealer network also continued to grow due to M.T.H. brand name recognition, as well as their presence at train shows and catalog circulation. Previously it was the tinplate collector that was familiar with the M.T.H. name, but now M.T.H. offered the O gauge train collector an ever-growing selection of engines, and freight and passenger cars. M.T.H. was gaining a reputation for variety,

quality, and affordability. Mike's vision for the model railroad enthusiast was becoming a reality.

Variety, Quality, Affordability, Innovation, and Expansion

M.T.H. undoubtedly was leading a revolution in the model train business. And they, in partnership with Samhongsa, were developing new products and getting them on the market at a pace that had never been seen before in the O gauge hobby.

As Mike continually kept his ears open in the marketplace, it became apparent that hobbyists and dealers greatly desired quality sound systems for their locomotives. M.T.H. established a relationship with QSI, Inc., a company that specializes in developing and producing toy train sound systems. M.T.H. purchased a supply of QSI components to be installed as an after-market enhancement. Then, the die-cast Challenger became the first product that incorporated the ProtoSound® System.

In 1995, M.T.H. continued to expand its product line. M.T.H. introduced an entirely new line of products – the landmark RailKing® Line. M.T.H. had been a player in the high-end market with their Premier Line of products, but with the introduction of the RailKing Line, M.T.H. was now able to provide quality products to the O-31/O-27 O gauge market. This was ideal for the model railroaders who had limited space and limited funds for their hobby, as well as entry level or casual collectors. The RailKing Line has allowed M.T.H. to further its mission to provide quality, affordable, family-oriented entertainment to new markets.

The first RailKing products were the New York Central and Santa Fe 4-8-2 L-3 Mohawk, the Pennsylvania GG-1, along with many freight cars. When the line was first introduced, it was fairly small. However, as train enthusiasts caught on to the outstanding quality and value of the line, it gained immense popularity and, by 1998, was placed first in the M.T.H. catalog. By 2000, the line was so large it had its own separate catalog! M.T.H. had hit another home run with the RailKing Line, which played a key role in the doubling of the O gauge market over the first seven years of M.T.H.'s participation in O gauge.

Steaming Down the Tracks

M.T.H. Electric Trains was well on its way to prominence in the O gauge hobby. Consumers all across the country were snapping up the many trains and accessories as the word spread about the quality and variety of the items produced by M.T.H.. Over the next several years, releases came at an almost staggering pace. The table beginning on page 13 highlights many of the milestones during this time.

1996

RailKing Challenger

The Challenger was once again a milestone for M.T.H.. It was the first-ever articulated steamer able to negotiate the O-31 curves found on many smaller train layouts.

RailTown Buildings

First fully assembled and painted buildings produced by M.T.H..

Tinplate Traditions

M.T.H. continued production of Standard Gauge after a brief absence. Along with the RailKing and Premier Lines, this became M.T.H.'s third line of trains offered.

Passenger Station Announcements and Freight Yard Sounds

For the first time ProtoSounds® includes the sounds of passenger trains arriving and departing a station or a freight train arriving in a yard.

1997

RailKing Ready-To-Run™ Train Sets

Though M.T.H. had been offering boxed sets, the Ready-To-Run sets marked the first time they included a transformer and track. This was also the introduction of the RiteTrax Track System – soon renamed RealTrax.

RealTrax™ Track System

This innovation is an easy-to-use, snap-together track system with a built-in roadbed. It is perfect for those who don't have permanent layouts, as it is easy to assemble while keeping carpet clean.

M.T.H.'s first operating accessory, the Sinclair Gas Station complete with moving car and sounds.

Sinclair Operating Gas Station

M.T.H.'s first operating accessory, complete with the sound of a 57 Chevy pulling out of the garage to a gas pump. Other operating accessories, such as the Fire Station and Car Wash, were soon to follow.

Premier Big Boy

The largest steam engine ever produced in real life was finally available in die-cast for the first time in O gauge.

The UL Approved 400 Watt Z-4000 Transformer

Z-4000 Transformer

The Spring 1997 Catalog featured, for the first time, the Z-2000 transformer. It eventually became the Z-4000 through enhancements and modifications. The Z-4000 was O gauge's first-ever, UL-approved, high-powered transformer and was a major landmark in M.T.H.'s technological developments.

The current headquarters of M.T.H. Electric Trains in Columbia, Maryland

M.T.H.'s Move

With the incredible expansion of M.T.H.'s product line and the immense amount of business taking place, adequate space was once again becoming an issue. On November 6, 1997, M.T.H. celebrated the official grand opening of its new headquarters building at 7020 Columbia Gateway Drive in Columbia, Maryland. This is the home of M.T.H. today.

1998

Premier DD40X Centennial

The largest diesel engine ever produced in real life was finally available for the first time in O gauge.

RealTrax Switches

M.T.H. introduced its own line of switches. The switches were much more reliable and operated better than the switches that were previously on the market, so they were very well received by hobbyists.

M.T.H. Railroaders Club

Club members receive the regular The Crossing Gate® newsletter, which keeps them current on M.T.H. products. Members also receive all catalogs and have the opportunity to purchase special promotional products.In addition, Club members have access to a special area on the M.T.H. Web site where they can even create their own Web pages showcasing their trains and layouts.

1999

RailWare CD-ROM

M.T.H. was the first train manufacturer to offer a CD-ROM with all of their train sets. RailWare™, as it is called, included the RR-Track Layout Design Software, video clips, and other important information for first-time buyers.

Premier Centipede

This 12-axle diesel engine was another first in O gauge for M.T.H..

ScaleTrax™

Billed as the "ultimate solution for the detail-oriented, 3-rail, scale model railroader," this track system featured individual ties along with the lowest profile and maximum scale accuracy.

Z-4000 Remote Commander™	First listed in the 1999 Volume III catalog, the Remote Commander allowed M.T.H. operators the freedom to walk anywhere around their layout and stay in complete control of their trains.
Product Locator System (PLS)	The Product Locator System is a part of the M.T.H. Electric Trains web site that allows users to search inventories of M.T.H. Dealers across the country for past produced products. The PLS prevents catalogs from becoming dated as both newcomers and established enthusiasts have the tool to find that particular item they have been looking for.

2000

Digital Command System (DCS)	The most significant announcement in M.T.H. history was first introduced the 2000 Volume II catalog. That was the introduction of ProtoSound 2.0 with a Digital Command System (DCS) and Loco-Sound™. Loco-Sound is the low-cost alternative that allows even inexpensive train sets to have robust locomotive sounds. ProtoSound 2.0 provides the most realistic sound that has ever been available before and also includes many new operational features such as controllable smoke output, one mph increment speed control, and the ability to individually command each train. The most significant feature of the DCS is that it is the first fully compatible command system in O gauge railroading – operating a Lionel train in command mode, an M.T.H. train in DCS command mode, and any other conventional train at the same time on the same track.

2001

RailKing Rugged Rails™ Series	First appearing in the 2001 Volume I catalog, these competitively priced, yet durable, freight cars were aimed specifically at entry-level hobbyists. The cars came in several models allowing hobbyists to easily expand their fleets.
RailKing One-Gauge	M.T.H. announces its entry into another gauge of model trains – Gauge 1. Several diesel and steam engines, all equipped with ProtoSound 2.0 highlighted the initial offerings, as more items followed in subsequent catalogs.
RealTrax Catenary System	Authentic-looking catenary poles and wires allow model railroaders the opportunity to set up realistic looking and operating systems for their electric locomotives (such as the GG-1).

The Toy Train Revolution

From its humble beginnings in Mike's childhood home, to the huge enterprise housed in the 125,000-square-foot space on Columbia Gateway Drive, M.T.H. has been the driving force in the O gauge field. With Mike Wolf's continued dedication to giving customers what they want, the future certainly looks very bright for the O gauge hobby.

CHAPTER 3

Planning Your Model Railroad

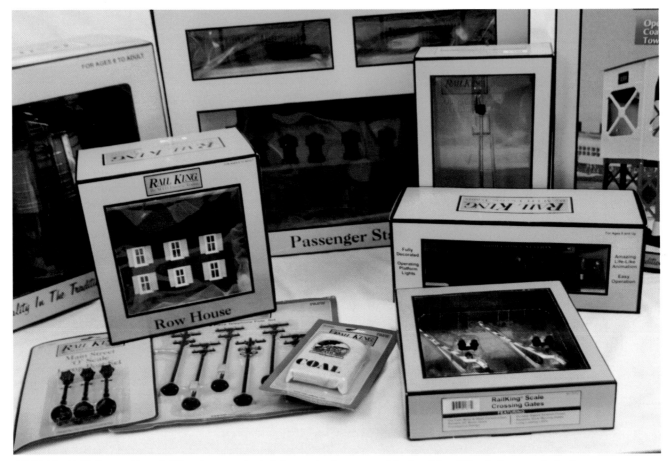

M.T.H. Electric Trains provides a full line of accessories to help you plan for your model railroad. In addition to these products, there are many other factors you will want to take into consideration when planning your layout.

Whether you are brand new to the hobby of model railroading with M.T.H. Electric Trains, or a seasoned veteran, it's a good idea to take the time to do some planning before jumping into the construction of your model railroad layout. It's true that many model railroaders don't know exactly *what* to plan for, so they give very little, if any, forethought to this part of the process. But a little bit of time invested now will reap many rewards later on – and save you a few headaches along the way.

This chapter will deal with several important aspects of planning your layout. While it is not an exhaustive list, it can help guide you through some of the steps you can take to build your layout. The hope is that this chapter will give you ideas you may want to use – or encourage you to expand upon the ideas that you already have. The underlying goal is to create a concept of your layout before the first piece of track is put down on the train table.

Keep in mind that, although you do need to spend some time planning, once you begin construction, you will probably be making adjustments and changes along the way. Flexibility is key and should be viewed as part of the whole process – and part of the fun!

Space Considerations

A layout can be built nearly anywhere that you have enough room. How about building it in the basement, attic, garage, or spare bedroom? There are also other options. I have seen many model railroaders come up with some very ingenious solutions as to where to place their model train layout. Here is a list of some of the most common locations for layouts, along with positives and negatives for each.

Location	Positives	Negatives
Basement	Plenty of room.	Can possibly flood. Moisture and/or dampness can be a problem.
Attic	Plenty of room.	Hot/cold temperature extremes. Sometimes height is limited.
Garage	Large space.	Hot/cold temperature extremes. Can be dusty and dirty.
Spare Bedroom	Climate control is good.	Working space can be limited. May need the room later on for other uses.

The dining room area was the location chosen for the Santa Fe Raton Pass Railroad. Shelves to display trains along with pictures add to the railroad atmosphere of the new "train room."

Some people have the luxury to actually have a couple of choices for the placement of a model railroad layout. If this is your case, create a list of them on a sheet of paper. For each area, write down the positives and negatives, along with any other factors that are specific to that location. Seeing all the factors at once may help you make a better final decision.

If your layout space is limited, don't get discouraged; you can still have a realistic and very enjoyable model railroad in a small space. With a few tricks and some creative construction, you can easily build a realistic and enjoyable model train layout. You'll see this as we construct the Santa Fe Raton Pass Railroad step-by-step through the remainder of this book … in a small, four foot by eight-foot area.

The Purpose of Your Layout

Perhaps because the purpose of a layout seems so obvious, many model railroaders don't give it much thought. If you do, though, you'll broaden the scope of your layout beyond a place to just run your trains around and around – such a layout can soon lead to what I call "circle-burnout." As much as you may enjoy running your M.T.H. Electric Trains, with all the neat features such as synchronized chuffing, ProtoSmoke on the steam engines, and the Cab Chatter on the diesels, eventually some of the excitement may start to wear off. This is why it is very important during the planning stage to develop a sense of purpose for your railroad to prevent "circle-burnout."

The best place to start is to examine real railroads and how they operate. Since the goal is to create a realistic model railroad, this aspect of planning is extremely vital. You may be asking yourself at this point, "How can I emulate a real railroad – one that has thousands of miles of track – on a sheet of plywood?" The answer is simply that you can't. Still, this doesn't stop us from imitating a small portion of the real thing on our model railroad layout, with imagination to fill in the rest. This technique is often referred to as selective compression. We will have to make sacrifices in what we want to include and what we need to cut out. The goal is to maintain as much realism as possible in what we do create. This notion is referred to as being prototypical, and while it may sound difficult, it definitely can be done.

A track plan is a track plan, right? Not exactly. Is an automobile just an automobile? Yes – and no: the broad heading of automobiles can be broken down into different categories, such as cars, trucks, SUVs, and vans. The same breakdown into cate-gories applies to track plans. As different as most model train layouts appear to be, they usually fall into one of several main categories; here is a list of the main types of track plans used by model rail-roaders:

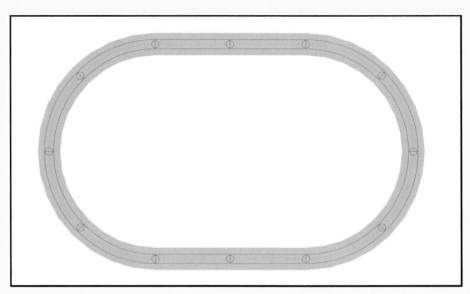

Closed Loop

This is arguably the most popular type; its truest form is a simple circle or oval. Almost all of the M.T.H. RailKing Ready-To-Run starter sets come with track to create this type of configuration. Many first-time model railroaders utilize this type because it is the simplest track plan for running their trains. The major advantage of it is that it allows you to run your trains continuously.

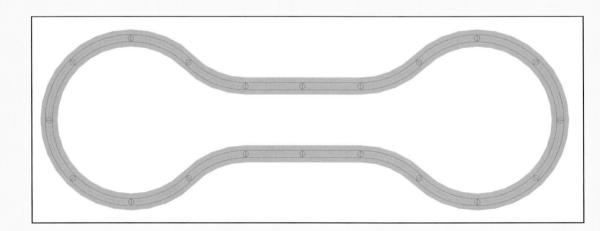

Dogbone

Another popular type of track plan involves two closed loops that have been joined together, allowing for continuous train operation. A varia-tion on this type involves the use of switches with a single track con-necting the two loops.

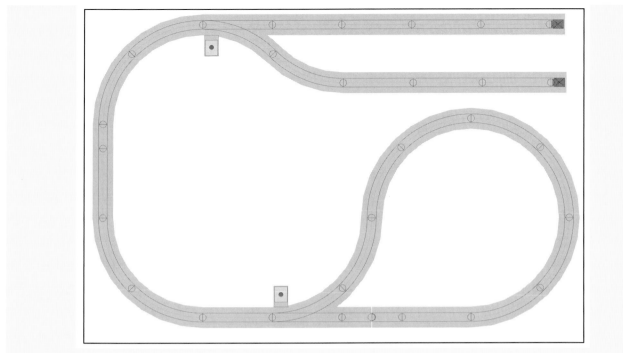

Out-and-Back

This type of track plan is usually employed where larger spaces are available for a layout. It involves having a yard (or point) at one end and a closed loop at the other end. Trains start in the yard, travel out to the loop, and return to the yard.

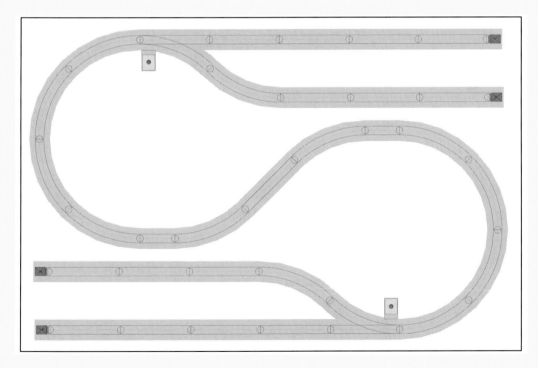

Point-to-Point

One of the less modeled types of track plans is the point-to-point. Trains are made in one yard (or point) and then travel over the layout to the other yard (or point). In real life, this is how all railroads actually operate. However, due to space limitations on our model railroad layouts, we can rarely afford to make our track plans this way. This type of track plan does not allow for continual running.

Almost all layout track plans fall into one of the four categories, but it is important to note that these four types are simply basic layouts upon which you can build. For example, you could take a closed loop and fold it over to create a figure eight by adding a M.T.H. Figure 8 Layout Builder (Item 40-1025). The addition of a M.T.H. Left- or Right-Hand Track Siding (Item 40-1026 or 40-1027) would soon make this track plan look far different than the basic closed loop. The great part is that whatever you decide to do, M.T.H. allows you to easily expand through a wide selection of RealTrax products to meet your needs.

For the purpose of the Santa Fe Raton Pass Railroad, I chose to use a closed loop track plan. I plan to incorporate a divider section to help split the layout into the two replicas of the real-life towns of Raton, New Mexico, and Trinidad, Colorado. The closed loop will also help make the layout seem bigger than it really is, when the train disappears in the tunnel from one town to the next. Additionally, this type of setup (with two towns) will provide for more realistic train operations, as you will see in the chapter titled "The Dispatcher Game" (page 109).

The next chapter will discuss creating and designing track plans using the *RR-Track Layout Design Software* that is provided on the M.T.H. RailWare CD-ROM for your personal computer.

LAYOUT THEMES

Another aspect to consider when planning your model railroad is a layout theme. A theme is simply a focus on a particular function of a real railroad – such as a large passenger station, or coal mining facility. Layouts with a large amount of space usually have several themes incorporated into them, while those with limited space may focus on only one or two. The chart illustrates some of the different types of themes that you can incorporate into your M.T.H. layout:

Passenger Trains	Erect a large passenger station, such as the M.T.H. Passenger Station, with Dual Platforms (Item 30-9050).
Coal/Mining	Build a coal mine using the M.T.H. Operating Coal Tower (Item 30-9043) with RailKing Hoppers and Operating Dump Cars to haul coal and/or ore.
Lumber/Logging	In this logging camp setup, logs are loaded on a M.T.H. RailKing Log Dump Car and routed to an Operating Saw Mill (Item 30-9122).
Grain/Farming	Utilize M.T.H. Covered Hoppers and Refrigerated Cars to haul grain and other farm produce to market.
Cattle/Livestock	M.T.H. RailKing Stock Cars can move livestock to a designated location.
Oil/Gas	Use M.T.H. RailKing Tank Cars to move petroleum from an Oil Derrick (Item 30-9059) to an Operating Storage Tank and Station (Items 30-9116 and 30-9117).
Trolley	Town setting using M.T.H. PCC and Brill Trolleys among RailTown Buildings.
Subway	Set up an urban area with M.T.H. RailKing Subway Sets.
General Freight	Use M.T.H. RailKing Boxcars to move freight to and from an Operating Transfer Dock (Item 30-9110) to other locations on the layout.
Civil War/Old West	The M.T.H. RailKing Central Pacific Jupiter (Item 30-1228) or Union Pacific 4-4-0 (30-1229) Steam Engine would look great in this genre of model railroading.

If you have a particular interest in one aspect of railroading, choosing one specific theme may be well suited for you … as it was for my father-in-law. He grew up in Oklahoma where oil wells and refineries were quite plentiful. As an adult, he has been collecting many of the tank cars that M.T.H. has produced in its RailKing line, and is planning to incorporate a large refinery, reminiscent of those from his childhood, into his model railroad layout.

Most model railroads pull several themes together into the layout. I strongly suggest that you try to do this even if your space is limited, as it creates greater operating possibilities. For the Santa Fe Raton Pass Railroad, I utilized the coal mine, cattle pen/meat packing, lumber/milling, and general freight transport themes.

Realism Considerations

In attempting to make your layout as realistic as possible, consider these aspects before construction begins:

Location

Is your layout going to have a real life location that it is modeled after? The Santa Fe Raton Pass Railroad was modeled after the actual location on the Colorado and New Mexico state border. Some may have different railroad memories or childhood experiences; some may have grown up close to the famous Horseshoe Curve, while others grew up seeing beautiful steam engines traverse the coast of California. Model railroaders will often build based on memories of their youth and the trains operating then.

Tony Lash, whose phenomenal layout is featured in the last chapter of this book, is a great example. In his youth, Tony got to ride with his grandfather in the cab of the large Y6b articulated steam engines of the Norfolk and Western Railroad. As a result, many of the scenes and locations on Tony's layout are replicas of his memories from his childhood.

You don't have to stick to following a real railroad; you can combine locations by taking the best together to make up your own. You can even choose to totally make up the location. This type of model railroading is called "freelancing" and is quite popular. The key point to remember is that it is your layout and you can do whatever you want.

Time Period

The time period is often overlooked when making a realistic model railroad. Time period simply refers to the point in time you are trying to capture on your layout. It also is referred to by many as the "era" of railroading. There are several eras that most model railroads fall into as far as their period is concerned. They are listed in the chart below:

When considering which time period to model on your layout, you may want to choose to do more than one. This is what I did on the Santa Fe Raton Pass Railroad, as I like to operate both the Transition and Modern Diesel Eras. For the Transition Era, I simply run steam engines and early diesels such as F3s. I also use earlier types of rolling stock to keep in accordance with this particular time period. For the Modern Diesel Era, I run Dash-8s and Genesis Diesel Engines along with modern rolling stock, such as Intermodel Stack Cars, Center Flow Covered Hoppers, and Modern Tank Cars. Operating your trains with appropriate equipment for the particular era or railroading adds authenticity and realism to your model railroad.

RAILROAD ERAS	
Early Steam	This era includes Civil War and other early railroading. Typical engines of the time period include 4-4-0 and 4-6-0 wheel arrangements such as the M.T.H. RailKing Denver and Rio Grande Ten-Wheeler (Item 30-1160). The time period is generally thought to range from the beginning of steam engines until roughly 1900.
Steam	Though this period can cover all steam engines, it generally refers to those made after 1900, and up until the time that diesels were first introduced. M.T.H. offers a wide array of possibilities in this category.
Transition	The time period in which diesels began to come on to the scene, up until steam engines were completely phased out, is the transition era. It is generally from the late 1930s up until the late 1950s. This era is a favorite among model railroaders, as it allows both types of engines to be run side by side and remain realistic according to history.

Early Diesel	Refers to the time from the 1950s to 1980s. Once again, M.T.H. Electric Trains has many engines available from this time period. Some will even break this period down further by identifying "1st and 2nd Generation" diesel engines.
Modern Diesel	Typically, this period started in the 1980s and goes up to the present. It largely consists of big, powerful, modern diesels with long-unit trains carrying loads such as intermodel containers, piggyback trailers, grain, oil/petroleum, and coal along with mixed freight. This period is sometimes referred to as "3rd generation" diesel.
Electric	This particular era is different from all the others in that it has a large time span, which covers several of the other groups listed. Electrics began showing up in the steam period and are still in use throughout the world today. M.T.H. Electric Trains offers many choices in this area from GG1s to Trolleys to Subway Cars.

Research Real Railroads

Many model railroaders start by throwing some track on the table and running their trains. Building your layout in this way is much like building a house without a foundation – sure, the trains will run, but how will they compare to trains in real life? I understand that for some, the joy of just running trains is enough. I enjoy "just running trains," too, but I have found my enjoyment increases greatly when I take it a step further and try to make my layout work as much as possible like a real-life railroad.

One of the best pieces of advice that I can give to beginning model railroaders who seek realistic train layouts is to do a little research on real railroads. Mind you, it doesn't have to be a lot, but some research can provide invaluable information as you plan, build, and operate your railroad empire. I have personally found a great deal of enjoyment in studying the Santa Fe Railroad in general and specifically the Raton Pass located between the towns of Trinidad, Colorado, and Raton, New Mexico. My research has given me a great sense of ownership of my layout (see sidebar on Santa Fe Raton Pass history), and increased my expertise overall. Even though our model railroads will never be able to recreate the real thing, gaining knowledge helps to fill in the "gaps" where our model railroads fall short.

For some, researching real railroads is a pleasant hobby in itself. For others, the thought of research may not sound very appealing, filled with images of running to the library and checking out ten large books on real railroads and then going home to spend countless hours poring through page after page into the wee hours of the night about the master brake cylinders on the four-wheel trailing trucks of steam engines. I am not insisting on research of this kind. Instead, try to keep it fun. Your research can be as simple as buying or borrowing a video and watching it or browsing a few Web pages on the Internet. There are many resources out there for model railroaders, and you can choose among the ones that best suit you. The following list provides several sources to get you started in researching the real railroads:

Learning about real railroads can be a lot of fun. There are many sources available to the model railroader filled with interesting facts and information.

Books	Books are the most prominent and plentiful source for information on real railroads. Books range from small to big and thick to thin. Some can be very broad in their subject content, while others are very specific. The key here is that you have many choices. You may want to start out with one or two books and just browse through them, reading what interests you. Good sources for finding books are book stores, your local library, hobby shops, and train meets/shows.
Videos	Train videos are a personal favorite of mine. Though they don't always go to the same depths books often do, there is something to be said for seeing footage of trains in action – especially for those of us who didn't grow up in the steam era. Some producers of train videos include: Pentrex: **www.pentrex.com** Railway Productions: **www.railwayproductions.com** Green Frog Productions: **www.greenfrog.com** Sunday River Productions: **www.sundayriverproductions.com** Machines of Iron: **www.machinesofiron.net**
Internet	As each day goes by, more and more information is available on the Internet. Many book and video production companies have Web sites you can visit and even purchase items from directly. However, if you know how to use a search engine such as Google (www.google.com) or Yahoo (www.yahoo.com), then you will soon find that the Internet is also a great source of information for researching real railroads from the actual railroad Web sites, to individual train enthusiasts' home pages.
Magazines	Regularly published magazines such as Trains and Classic Trains provide a great amount of information that model railroaders can utilize in planning realistic layouts.
Observation	Observe your local railroad. Watching trains and seeing the type of engines and rolling stock can be very useful. If you happen to live close to a small train yard or an area with a lot of train traffic, this can be a very exciting "field trip" to help you learn more about real railroads.

Planning for Operation

Real railroads operate with a purpose – to move people and freight from location to location in a timely manner. But if, as mentioned earlier, you set up a plain loop of track, you may end up experiencing "circle burnout" at some point down the line. To combat this, build realistic operational opportunities into your layout design. The varied operating sessions with your trains will give you much greater enjoyment, and keeps the model railroading experience exciting.

Another issue to consider is the M.T.H. Digital Command System (DCS). DCS brings to O gauge model railroading astounding capabilities never before seen in the hobby through numerous features that are available no matter what kind of layout you build. However, to take full advantage of these remarkable features, you may want to plan your model railroad specifically with DCS in mind. For an example, if you were to plan a layout with few or no industrial sidings to drop off boxcars and other types of freight cars, you wouldn't have much of an opportunity to utilize the Proto-Couplers on your M.T.H. engine, throw a switch directly through the DCS Remote, or initiate the exciting Freight Yard Sounds sequence. In other words, you'd miss all the realistic operations fun to be had with the DCS!

Create a Transportation System

When creating a transportation system, don't concentrate too much on trains; not every square inch of your model railroad needs to have track on it. Remember, real railroads move people and freight from one location to another in order to make a profit. When you plan and design your model railroad, you must not only pay attention to the trains and where they will run, but also the businesses and industries they will serve. There has to be a place to deliver and pick up all those goods and products ... so you will need to add sidings to serve these businesses, allowing the railroad to deliver boxcars, refrigerat-

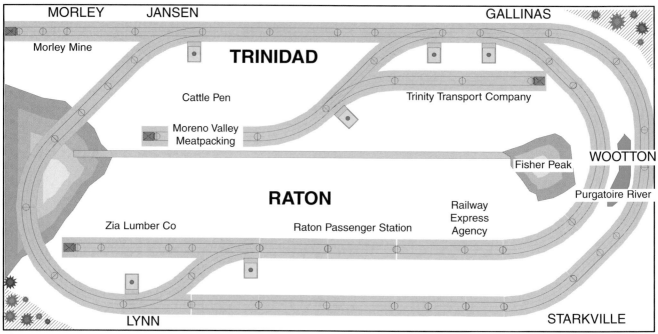

On the Santa Fe Raton Pass Railroad I named not only the location of industries, but also included several town names. Though they don't have actual buildings in some of these locations, they help to give a sense of place to the layout and make it seem larger.

ed cars, hoppers, and other types of rolling stock to them. Don't forget that this same rolling stock eventually will have to be picked up later on and returned, or possibly delivered to another location. Creating a realistic transportation system can be a lot of fun (as you will see in the "The Dispatcher Game," page 109).

In planning the Santa Fe Raton Pass Railroad, I really wanted to allow for many options in operating trains, so I incorporated three sidings and six different industries into the plan. Additional items such as stations and water towers further add to the options for operation. I figured this would keep me pretty busy switching cars around while waiting for the *Super Chief* hotshot passenger train to come roaring into town for a quick stop before heading on its way again!

One Track or Two?

Real railroads have mainlines, comparable to the highways that our cars travel upon. Mainlines are the key path that most of the regularly scheduled trains run on, and they can consist of one, two, and even three tracks – much like our one, two, and three lane highways.

In planning your layout for operation, you'll need to decide how many mainline tracks you will need. In most cases, it will be two (one if space is limited). Many model railroaders like to have two mainlines so that multiple trains can run easily at the same time. However, two tracks may not always be suitable for a

couple of reasons. First, we need to look at the real railroad that we are attempting to emulate: does it have a single or double track mainline – or a mixture? Secondly, if space for the layout is limited, we may face the tough choice of deciding between a second mainline track, and multiple sidings with several industries. If your layout space is limited, I would recommend going with the single track and several industries for your railroad to serve. Such a choice may seem like a sacrifice, but it will be well worth it when it comes to running your trains and operating them like a real railroad, because there will be actual locations for rolling stock to go to and from.

On the Santa Fe Raton Pass Railroad, I used a single-track mainline because I wanted the maximum amount of industry sidings that I could get. I did manage to fit a second mainline around part of the layout to allow trains to pass one another during operation. It worked out perfectly, and it's realistic: the real Raton Pass currently has part single and part double mainline between Raton and Trinidad. I also like the single track mainline for its operating challenges … some ingenuity is called for when developing solutions for certain situations, such as when two trains traverse over the pass in opposite directions. It definitely makes for some very exciting operations!

Name Every Location

It is important to name every location on the layout. Upon first thought, this task may not seem that vital, but it really is just the opposite. When you give names to locations on your model railroad, you are also giving that location a reason to exist and a sense of purpose. Furthermore, since we can't possibly model the vast amount of space that real railroads possess, defining locations, even when right next to each other, helps to create a sense of distance between the two points. This virtual distance makes your layout seem larger than it really is.

Another good reason for naming locations on your model railroad is that your M.T.H. Electric Trains will have places to go to and from. This is especially fun when you use the Digital Command System's Proto-Cast feature to announce stations and locations for arriving and departing trains. Even if you are just operating trains with a friend or family member, location names will allow you to call out your train's progress to one another: "I'm over here at the Wootton Curve," or "I'm waiting for the freight to pass at the Gallinas switch."

When naming locations, you really have three choices: make up a fictional name, utilize the research you did by giving the location the corresponding name of an actual place along the railroad, or a combination of the first two. For the Santa Fe Raton Pass Railroad I chose the last option, as I named a few items for people and places that have special meaning to me. Whatever you choose, just remember to name as much as possible, from towns and stations to switches, industries, sidings, roads, rivers, hills, and even mountains. Have fun with this! I know that I certainly did, as you can see some of the names of locations on the schematic of the Santa Fe Raton Pass Railroad. (And, as you will see later, naming locations will play a big key in the "Dispatcher Game," on page 109.)

Tying It All Together

Taking the time to plan your model railroad layout might seem like extra time and work. Still, the process of doing a little research and planning can be very enjoyable. And, it's almost guaranteed that setting the time aside before you begin to build will pay big dividends, leading to long-lasting satisfaction with your model railroad.

As you go about this phase, keep in mind that the ideas outlined in this chapter are intended to stimulate your planning process. Your personal preferences, above all else, are the most important – doing what you like because it is your railroad. Let me remind you to remain flexible. Your plans will evolve from the beginning to the completion of your model railroad layout. Don't let this get you down if it happens, but rather "roll with the changes," as the old saying goes. Staying flexible will make the process much more enjoyable for you – and that's what model railroading with M.T.H. Electric Trains is all about.

One of the benefits of doing a little research on real railroads is finding out interesting facts. For example, during WWII, the Santa Fe bought several Y3 articulated steam engines (very similar to the Y6b pictured) from the Norfolk & Western to help haul coal over Raton Pass.

A History of Santa Fe's Raton Pass

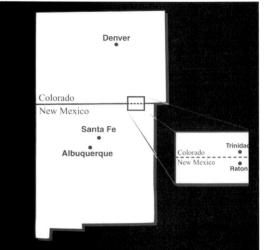

The Atchison, Topeka, and Santa Fe Railway – or the Santa Fe, as it has come to be known – is one of the classic American railroads. From its humble beginnings in 1860 in the state of Kansas, led by founder Cyrus K. Holliday, the Santa Fe grew well beyond expectations by stretching all the way from Chicago to Los Angeles and Galveston (on the Gulf of Mexico) to San Francisco. At one point in 1931, the Santa Fe had amassed a total of 13,568 miles of track, which made it the largest railroad in the country at that time.

One of the most illustrious points on the Santa Fe is Raton Pass (pronounced RA-tone), located between Raton, New Mexico, and Trinidad, Colorado. Besides the grandeur of the mountainous terrain offering many impressive views, Raton Pass also happens to be the highest point on the entire railroad, rising to an altitude of 7,588 feet or roughly a mile and half above sea level. It contains some of the steepest railroad grade elevation changes in the United States, topping out at 3.5 percent.

Though today's Raton Pass is owned and operated by the BNSF Railroad from the resulting merger in 1995 of the Santa Fe and Burlington Northern Railroads, the legacy and rich history of this part of the line will forever serve as a reminder of the challenges and adventures of the early railroaders. How the Raton Pass came to be is quite an amazing story, enhancing the legacy of the Santa Fe Railway.

In its infancy, the Santa Fe quickly laid rails across the plains of Kansas, reaching the Colorado border in 1872. Once there, the Santa Fe faced a stiff competitor in the Denver & Rio Grande Railroad. Like the Santa Fe, the Denver & Rio Grande had aspirations of expanding their rails into New Mexico, and both railroads knew that Raton Pass was the means to get there. The problem was that there was only room for one line over the pass, and the situa-

tion was compounded by the toll road over Raton Pass – owned by a man named Dick Wootton.

Santa Fe's General Manager, William Barstow Strong, assembled a crew to head to Raton Pass and prepare to build a line across, using force if necessary. The race had begun. On February 26, 1878, civil engineers from both railroads – unaware of each other – rode a Denver & Rio Grande train to El Moro, Colorado – just a few miles away from the pass. While the Denver & Rio Grande crew retired for the night at the local hotel, the Santa Fe crew went right to work.

Lead by A.A. Robinson and William Ray Morley, the Santa Fe crew negotiated with Dick Wootton to purchase the right to build over the pass. Once the deal was completed, the crew members went right to work early that cold morning, shovels in one hand and guns in the other. The Denver & Rio Grande crew showed up just minutes afterwards, creating several tense moments. But in those days, possession was nine-tenths of the law, so the Santa Fe gained control of Raton Pass.

The work of building the rail line began in earnest several days later with the first Santa Fe train eventually entering New Mexico on December 7, 1878, via a switchback over Raton Pass. This allowed the drilling of the 2,041 foot tunnel from both ends. The tunnel was opened on September 1, 1879, and the switchback was then abandoned. In 1909, a second tunnel was completed to accommodate additional rail traffic. The original tunnel was abandoned in 1948, and completely plugged in 1953.

The Raton Pass is still in service by the BNSF Railroad. Though the rail traffic is significantly less than during its heyday, Raton Pass still sees several mixed freight, intermodal, and coal trains along with Amtrak's daily Southwest Chief passenger train.

Real railroad action on Raton Pass in mid 1990s. Photo by Rob Adelman.

Designing Track Plans Using RR-Track Layout Design Software

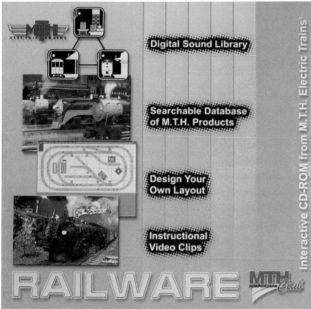

The RR-Track Layout Design Software is included with the M.T.H. Electric Trains RailWare CD-ROM.

Designing a track plan is a fun and exciting part of building your model railroad. It gives you the opportunity to take all of your creative ideas, along with the valuable information you gathered during your research, and pull them together to form something concrete and tangible – a track plan. You will find great enjoyment watching it transform from thought, to track plan, to reality.

Part of the fun of creating a track plan is the fact that you're the boss and you get to decide where each piece of track goes, as well as where buildings, accessories, and scenery (such as mountains and streams) are located. I will warn you, though, that you may find it to be so much fun that you will want to keep creating more and more track plans – especially when you see how easy it is to do with *RR-Track Layout Design Software* by R & S Enterprises. In fact, I recommend that you create a couple of different track plans to give yourself choices before you begin constructing your model railroad.

That was Then, This is Now

In years past, the only tools a model railroader had to design a track plan with was a pencil and some paper. Designing and drawing track plans by hand was a time consuming method that posed many problems, such as calculating for the correct sizing of objects, and whether the track would actually fit in the given area. On top of this, if the model railroader changed his mind numerous times, the paper would often tear due to the many eraser marks ... ruining the hard work and effort put into it. The model railroader had to start over from square one.

Today, you no longer have to struggle with these difficulties when designing a track plan for your M.T.H. Electric Trains. With a personal computer, you can use the M.T.H. RailWare CD-ROM. This CD contains the RR-Track Layout Design Software by R & S Enterprises – a sort of electronic sheet of graph paper to quickly and easily plan your model railroad layout.

Why Use RR-Track Layout Design Software?

There are numerous advantages to using RR-Track Layout Design software to create your model railroad track plan:

- Layout plan files are easy to maintain without the use of paper or clumsy templates.

- Pre-done pieces of track and accessories mean you don't have to re-create them each time, giving you the ability to easily re-configure them if you change your mind.

- You can move and delete track pieces quickly and easily without any annoying eraser marks.

- Track placement accuracy: You know exactly where the track goes and if it will fit in any given location on your layout.

- You can produce a list of the quantity and type of every single piece of track and accessories placed on the layout.

- You can quickly copy and paste items in the layout or from one layout file to another.

- The user interface and consistency between tasks make it easy to learn how to use.

How Do I Get the RR-Track Layout Design Software?

If you purchased M.T.H. Electric Trains Ready-To-Run Set, you have already discovered that M.T.H. includes a copy of the RailWare CD-ROM in every set. Additionally, if you join the M.T.H. Railroaders Club, one of the benefits includes receiving the RailWare CD-ROM as part of your membership. You can purchase the M.T.H. Model Railroaders Handbook (Item 60-1355, $14.95 MSRP), which includes the M.T.H. RailWare CD-ROM, from the M.T.H. Electric Trains Web site at **www.mth-railking.com** or at your local hobby shop.

M.T.H. RAILWARE CD-ROM FEATURES

In addition to the RR-Track Layout Design Software, the M.T.H. RailWare CD-ROM is packed with many other useful and exciting items for the model railroader, including:

Item	Description
Collection Tracking Software	Whether you are just starting in the hobby or you are a seasoned veteran, knowing what you have in your collection is important. The software can be directly installed onto the hard drive of your personal computer to help you keep track of your M.T.H. Electric Trains.
M.T.H. History Database	Have you ever wanted to see a list of all the M.T.H. RailKing Steam Engines made in the Santa Fe roadname? You can with this handy feature, as it allows you to search through every item M.T.H. has ever produced. You can do searches by roadname, engine type, product line, and many more – even by product number if you have it. Besides the important information it stores, the database even shows a picture of each product.
Train Music	In the mood to hear a good, old-fashioned song about railroading? The M.T.H. RailWare CD-ROM has several from which to choose.
Electronic M.T.H. Catalogs	This feature allows you to view all past M.T.H. Electric Trains Catalogs in electronic format using the Adobe Acrobat PDF format.
Instructional Video Clips	Actual video clips demonstrating many topics including some of the new Digital Command System (DCS) features.
Digital ProtoSound® 2.0 and Loco-Sound® Sound Effects Library	Want to hear sample Passenger Station Announcements or Train Wreck sounds that come with your M.T.H. Electric Trains engines? Go right ahead; many samples are included for you on the M.T.H. RailWare CD-ROM.
Searchable Database of all M.T.H. Retailers	Did you get your M.T.H. Electric Trains Ready-To-Run Set as a gift and want to know who sells them in your area? Find an M.T.H. Retail Dealer quickly and easily with this feature.
RR-Track Layout Design Software User Manual	Electronic version of the manual containing information on all the features of RR-Track Layout Design Software. Comes in Adobe Acrobat .pdf file format.

Not Good with Computers?

Are you a little apprehensive about using a personal computer? Is all this talk about CD-ROMs and software making you uneasy? Try viewing the RR-Track Layout Design Software as an opportunity rather than an obstacle. The model railroading hobby has long been very family-oriented, and if you are unsure about using computers, this would be the perfect time to enlist help from a son or daughter – or maybe a niece, nephew, grandson, or granddaughter. Working on a track plan with their help can provide wonderful time together as you complete this task for your model railroad layout.

Using RR-Track Layout Design Software with a younger family member provides excellent opportunity for family time together.

RR-Track Layout Design Software System Requirements

In order to use the RR-Track Layout Design Software, your computer must meet the minimum requirements listed below:

- Windows 95 or later Operating System

- Pentium 100

- 16 MB RAM

- CD-ROM drive

- Sound card

- 640 x 480 monitor resolution

RR-Track Layout Design Software Tutorial

The rest of this chapter will deal with the steps involved in creating an M.T.H. RealTrax track plan using RR-Track Layout Design Software. By no means can this chapter serve as an exhaustive reference for using the countless features included in the package – such a reference would be the size of a book by itself! (A complete instruction manual is included on the RailWare CD-ROM.) Instead, this chapter is meant to get you up and running quickly and easily through very clear descriptions and concise steps, along with many screen shots from the computer to help you. Hopefully, you will see just how easy using RR-Track Layout Design Software is, along with the numerous benefits it offers over, and in place of, a plain piece of paper and pencil.

As you go through the following tutorial, keep in mind that, as with all Windows software applications, there is often more than one way to perform a task. For the sake of time and efficiency, though, I will usually only cover one way to perform each task.

Installing RR-Track Layout Design Software

The RR-Track Layout Design Software can be run directly from the M.T.H. RailWare CD-ROM, although you may find the performance inadequate. I recommend installing the software directly onto the hard drive of your personal computer. Use the following steps:

1. Place the M.T.H. RailWare CD-ROM in the CD-ROM player of your computer.

2. Within a few seconds the Autorun feature will engage, and you will see the following screen.

3. Click on the Install Track Layout Software link on the right side of the screen to start the Installation Wizard, which will walk you through the steps to install the software.

4. On the Welcome screen as shown below, click on the Continue button.

For the Select Setup Option screen, click on the Typical option and then click on the Continue button.

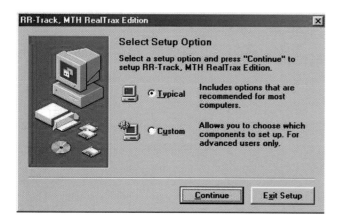

5. On the Select Application Folder screen, leave the default as it is (which should read c:\rrtrackm) and click on the Continue button.

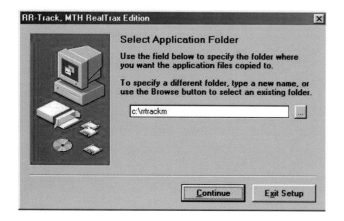

6. Installation of the software will begin and you will see a status bar indicating the progress, as shown below.

RR-Track, MTH RealTrax Edition

Extracting...
Description: rrtrackm.exe
From File: d:\rrsetup\setup.arv
To File: c:\rrtrackm\rrtrackm.exe
Completed: 32%
Cancel

7. On the Program Icons screen, leave the default, which should read RR-Track: M.T.H. RealTrax and click on the Continue button.

RR-Track, MTH RealTrax Edition

Program Icons

A set of icons will now be added to the following program group.

If you want to place the icons in a different group, type the name of the new or existing group below.

RR-Track: MTH RealTrax

Continue   Exit Setup

8. On the Setup was Successful! screen, click on the Close button, which closes the Installation Wizard.

RR-Track, MTH RealTrax Edition

Setup was successful

The installation is complete and the application has been properly set up.

Press "Close" to exit setup.

Continue   Close

The RR-Track Layout Design Software installation is now complete.

Starting RR-Track Layout Design Software
(when installed on your computer)

To start the RR-Track Layout Design Software application, perform the following steps:
1. Click on the Start button on the Task Bar.

2. Click on the Programs option on the menu.

3. Click on the RR-Track M.T.H. RealTrax option on the sub-menu to the right.

4. Click on the RR-Track M.T.H. Edition icon on the sub-menu to the right to launch the application.

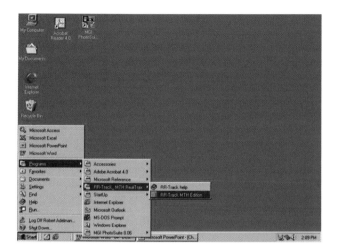

Working with Files

One of the great advantages of using a computer track layout design application is that you can save your work in an electronic format that you'll be able to re-open later to continue working on it. This section deals with the very important aspects of working with RR-Track files in the Windows operating environment using the New, Save, Close, Open, and Exit commands. If you are already adept at using computers, these commands should be very familiar to you. You may want to skip this section and go on to the one titled **Laying Track**.

Creating a New File

To create a new file to begin planning a layout, perform the following steps:
1. Click on the File menu.

2. In the Drawing Size dialog box, use the up and down selection arrows to change the width and depth of the layout size in feet and inches.

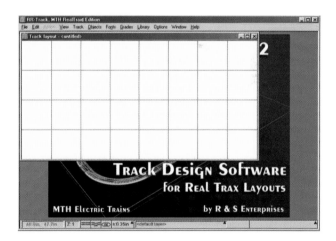

Note: If you are making a layout that is shaped other than a rectangle, use the overall total area for your length and width measurements. (As an example, for an L shaped layout using two 4x8 sheets of plywood tables, you would enter 12' width by 8' depth.)

3. When you have the correct sizes entered in the Drawing Size dialog box, click on the OK button. You now have a new layout file and are ready to start designing your model railroad layout.

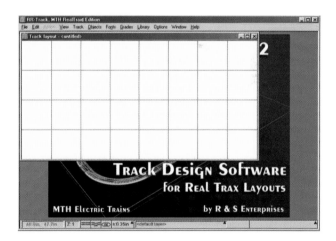

Note: Depending upon the size of your layout, the gridlines may appear closer together or farther apart. For best viewing results, click on the Maximize button of the layout file window. This will help the window fully utilize the available space on the monitor screen, making it easier for you to work.

Saving Files

One of the advantages of using RR-Track Layout Design Software is that it gives you the ability to save files on the computer for use later. I strongly urge you to perform this task before you begin to lay your first piece of track. To save your file, complete the following steps:

1. Click on the File menu.

2. Click on the Save As... option.

3. In the Save Track Layout dialog box you will have several choices to make.

4. Start by typing in the name of the file in the File Name text box. Try to keep the name short, and use only letters and numbers.

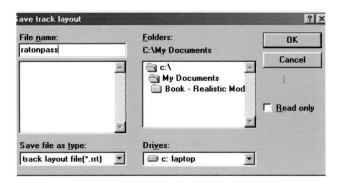

Note: You do not need to put the .rrt file extension on the end of the name of your file as the application will do this for you automatically when you save it.

5. To save to a different drive, such as a floppy disk or other hard drive, click on the drop-down menu in the lower right and select the drive you want.

6. To save the file in a different location on the selected drive, you will need to change directories. To do this, in the Folder list box, double-click on the c:\ (or whichever drive letter that is showing) directory. This will change the view and show all the directories on the given drive. You can then double-click on the directory that you want.

7. When you are done making your choices in the Save Track Layout dialog box, click on the OK button to save the file.

Note: As you work on designing your model railroad layout using RR-Track, it is a very good idea to save your work periodically – about every 5 to 10 minutes. You can perform this task quickly, either by using the keyboard shortcut of holding the Ctrl key and then pressing the S key, or clicking on the File menu and choosing Save.

Closing Files

When you are done working on a file, you can close it by following these steps:

1. Click on the File menu.

2. Click on the Close option.

Note: If you have not saved the file, you will be prompted to do so at this time.

Opening Files

If you want to open a file that already exists on the computer, perform the following steps:

1. Click on the File menu.

2. Click on the Open option.

3. In the Open Track Layout dialog box, click on the name of the file in the File Name list box. If the file is not listed there, you may need to change drives and directories. To accomplish this, move on to Step 4.

4. To look in a different drive such as a floppy disk or other hard drive, click on the drop down menu in the lower right and select the drive you want.

5. To look for the file in a different location on the selected drive, you will need to change directories. To do this, in the Folder list box, double-click on the c:\ (or whichever drive letter that is showing) directory. This will change the view and show all the directories on the given drive. You can then double-click on the directory that you want. The available RR-Track files for the selected directory will show in the File Name list box on the left.

6. Click on the OK button to open the file.

Exiting the RR-Track Application

When you have finished using the RR-Track Layout Design Software application, you can exit by performing these steps:

1. Click on the File menu.

2. Click on the Exit option.

Note: If you have not saved the file, you will be prompted to do so at this time.

Laying Track

Now you are ready to begin designing your model railroad layout. This section allows you to produce a basic track plan easily and efficiently.

Selecting the M.T.H. Track Library

By default, the M.T.H. Track Library should be selected when you first use the RR-Track Layout Design Software. In case it isn't, you will need to select it first in order to lay any M.T.H. RealTrax on your layout. To select the M.T.H. RealTrax library, follow these steps:

1. Click on the Library menu.

2. Click on M.T.H. RealTrax O (32mm).

Choosing and Placing the Track Type on the Layout

The first step in laying track is to choose a specific piece of M.T.H. RealTrax that you want to use. To access the M.T.H. RealTrax Library, where you will find all of the different track pieces that are available, follow these steps:

1. Click on the Track menu.

2. Click on the RealTrax Straights option.

3. Click on the 40-1001 10.0 option to select a 10-inch piece of RealTrax.

4. The mouse pointer will have a line attached with the word MOVE under it, as shown.

5. Move the mouse pointer to where you want the piece of track.

6. Click on the left mouse button to place the track. The piece of track will initially be red in color because it is still selected.

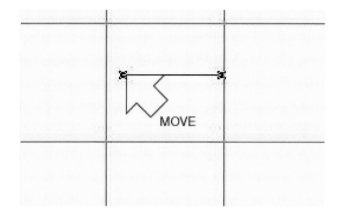

If you click your mouse in an open area away from the track, the track will become de-selected and turn gray.

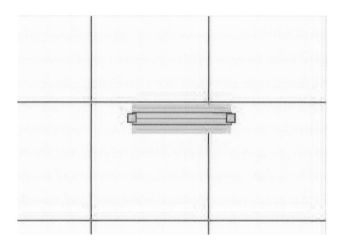

Moving Track

If the track is not in the correct location, or you decide later that it needs to be moved, you can do this easily by performing the following steps:

1. Move your mouse pointer so that it is on the piece of track you want to move.

2. Click and hold the mouse button down. The track will turn red (if it is not already) and your pointer will change to an arrow with the word MOVE underneath it.

3. Drag your mouse to the new location where you want to place the track.

4. Let go of the mouse button to place the track.

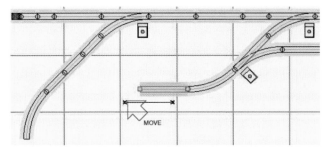

Note: To select several pieces of track to move at once, simply hold down your Shift key and click on each track individually to select them. As you do, each piece will turn red. Then click and drag one of the selected pieces of track to the new location and all others you selected will move with it.

Adding Track

To add another piece of RealTrax to your layout plan, simply follow the same steps in choosing and placing your first piece of track as listed above. However, this time the mouse pointer will change and have the words AUTO JOIN underneath it. If you try to place the track near another track, it will automatically connect the two (see the step below on Connecting Track for more information).

Note: If you want to add the same piece of RealTrax you just added in the previous step, simply double-click your mouse button in an open area of the track plan. A new piece of track will be attached to your mouse pointer. To place it on the layout, move your mouse to the correct location and click the left mouse button. This allows you to bypass going through the menus, which saves time when using the same piece of track repeatedly.

Connecting Track

The RR-Track Layout Design Software has a neat feature called Auto Join, which allows you to quickly and effortlessly join pieces of M.T.H. RealTrax on your track plan. The Auto Join feature works for both new pieces of track as well as ones already existing on the layout that need to be connected together. To connect two pieces of track together, follow these steps:

1. Select either a new piece of track or an existing one.
2. Move your mouse pointer with the piece of track attached so that the two ends of the tracks that you want to connect are either touching or very close to each other.

3. Let go of the mouse button.
4. The two pieces of track will snap together.

Disconnecting Track

If you decide you don't want two pieces of RealTrax connected anymore, you can quickly disconnect them. To do this, follow these steps:

1. Move your mouse pointer so that it is on the piece of track you want to disconnect.
2. Click and hold the mouse button down. The track will turn red (if it isn't red already) and your pointer will change to an arrow with the word MOVE underneath it.
3. Drag your mouse to the new location where you want to place the track.
4. Let go of the mouse button to place the track.

Note: If you don't move the piece of track far enough away, it will snap back into its original place.

Deleting Track

To remove of a piece of RealTrax that you no longer need on your model railroad track plan, you can delete it by performing these steps:

1. Click on the piece of track you want to delete.
2. Press the Delete key.

Closing a Loop of Track

One of the great features of RR-Track Layout Design Software is that, by default, it will automatically close a loop of track for you. This occurs when you attempt to put the last piece of track in place. The figure below shows an example from the Santa Fe Raton Pass Railroad track plan.

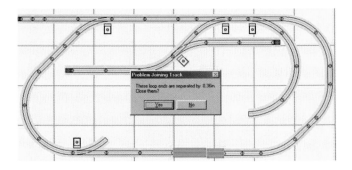

Notice that the loop is slightly off. If this is the case with your track plan, don't be alarmed; there is usually enough slack in the track to make minor adjustments so the tracks can connect. Later on, you will see a neat feature of RR-Track Layout Design Software, called Relax Selected Track Configuration, that will help to close this gap.

Note: If you want to turn this feature off, you can click on the Options menu and choose the Automatic Loop Closing option. The checkmark next to it will disappear indicating it has been turned off.

Rotating Track

When moving track around, you may find that it isn't positioned at the angle you need. If this is the case, you can rotate the piece of RealTrax using the following steps:

1. Click on the piece of track you want to rotate.

2. Move your mouse pointer just off the track and click on the right mouse button.

3. Choose the Rotate option in the short-cut menu that appears.

4. In the Rotate dialog box, click on the + or – buttons to adjust the angle.

5. The selected piece of track will move accordingly.

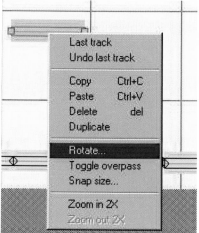

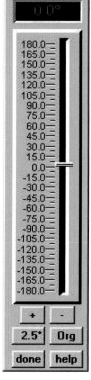

6. When the track is at the proper angle, click on the Done button in the Rotate dialog box.

Swapping Switch Machines

The switch machine mechanisms on the RealTrax switches protrude several inches away from the track. When designing a layout, this can cause a clearance problem with other pieces of track nearby. However, one of the terrific characteristics of the M.T.H. RealTrac Switch is that it allows the model railroader to easily change which side of the track the switch machine appears. The RR-Track Layout Design Software allows you do this, also. To make the change, do the following steps:

1. Click with your right mouse button on the turnout.

2. Click on the Swap Switch Machine checkbox.

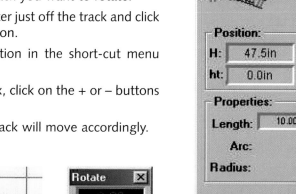

3. Click on the OK button.

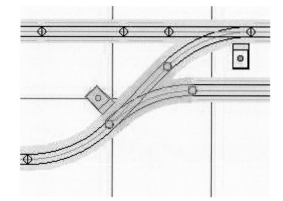

Showing Track Type on the Screen

When designing your model railroad layout, you may find it very useful to see what types of RealTrax you have used. To turn this feature on in your RR-Track Layout Design Software application, perform the following steps:

1. Click on the Options menu.

2. Click on the Label Track option.

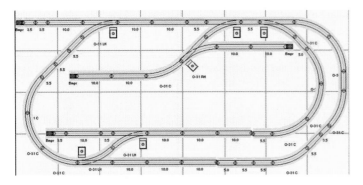

Adding Accessories

You will be happy to know that the process of adding accessories, such as Station Platforms, Crossing Gates, and Operating Gas Stations, to your model railroad layout involves virtually the same steps you used to place track. The consistency among different actions is one of the more valuable characteristics of the RR-Track Layout Design Software; learning one action will transfer over to other actions you perform.

Selecting the M.T.H. Accessory Library

The first step in placing any M.T.H. Accessory on your layout involves selecting the M.T.H. Accessory Library. To do this, follow these steps:

1. Click on the Library menu.
2. Click on M.T.H. Accessories.

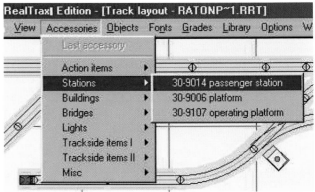

3. You should notice that the Track menu has now changed to the Accessories menu.

Note: If you want to switch back to the M.T.H. RealTrax Library to add more track, simply follow these same steps, but choose the M.T.H. RealTrax O Library instead of the M.T.H. Accessory Library.

Choosing an Accessory and Placing It on the Layout

The first step in placing an accessory is to choose a specific one that you want to use. By accessing the M.T.H. Accessory Library, you'll find all of the different track pieces that are available. To perform this task:

1. Click on the Accessories menu.
2. Click on the Station option.

3. Click on the 30-9014 Passenger Station.

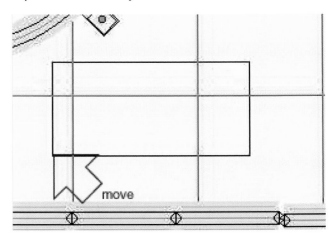

4. The mouse pointer will have a box outline attached with the word MOVE under it as shown below.

5. Move the mouse pointer to where you want to place the accessory.

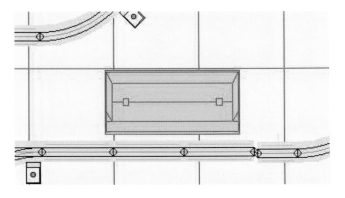

6. Click on the left mouse button to place the accessory. The accessory will initially be red in color because it is still selected.

If you click your mouse in an open area away from the accessory, the accessory will become de-selected and turn gray.

Moving an Accessory

If the accessory is not in the correct location, or you decide later that it needs to be moved, you can do this easily by following these steps:

1. Move your mouse pointer so that it is on the accessory you want to move.

2. Click and hold the mouse button down. The accessory will turn red (if not already) and your pointer will change to an arrow with the word MOVE underneath it.

3. Drag your mouse to the new location to place the accessory.

4. Let go of the mouse button to place the accessory.

Deleting an Accessory

To remove an accessory that you no longer need on your model railroad track plan, you can delete it by performing these steps:

1. Click on the accessory you want to delete.

2. Press the Delete key.

Adding Basic Shapes and Other Buildings

Over the last several years, M.T.H. Electric Trains has led the hobby in innovation, particularly with the wide range of new products. In the event that an accessory, such as a building, is not listed or if you create a structure on your own, you can still easily add this to your track plan. To do this, follow these steps:

1. Click on the Objects menu.

2. Click on the Buildings option.

3. Click on the Hip Roof Building option.

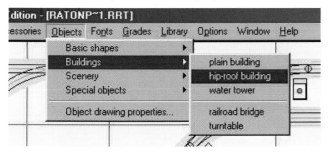

4. The mouse pointer will transform into a large plus with an x over it.

5. Move the mouse pointer to the location you want to place the building.

6. Click on the left mouse button and hold it down.

7. While holding the mouse button, drag the mouse downward and to the right. You will see the building start to appear and grow larger as you do.

8. When the building is sized correctly, let go of the mouse button.

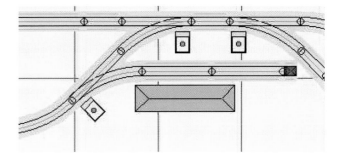

Note: If you need to move the new building, follow the same steps you would to move an accessory or track.

Resizing Basic Shapes and Other Buildings

After you place a basic shape or building, you may find that it is not the correct size. To resize it, perform these steps:

1. Click on the building to select it.

2. The building will turn red and have a very small red circle located on each corner.

3. Place your mouse pointer tip on one of the red corner circles.

4. Click and hold the left mouse button down.

5. Drag the mouse in the direction you desire to make the object bigger or smaller. The mouse pointer will transform into a white arrow with the word EDIT under it.

6. When the object is resized correctly, let go of the mouse button.

Adding Scenery

Within the RR-Track Layout Design Software application, you have the ability to also add a variety of scenery to your track plan, including mountains, boulders, embankments, varieties of trees, and ponds.

Trees and Boulders

To add these elements to your track plan, follow these steps:

1. Click on the Objects menu.

2. Click on the Scenery option.

3. Click on the Random Boulder option.

4. The mouse pointer will transform into a large plus with an x over it.

5. Move the mouse pointer to the location you want to place the boulder.

6. Click on the left mouse button and hold it down.

7. While holding the mouse button drag the mouse downward and to the right. You will see a circle outline start to appear and grow larger as you do.

8. When the boulder is sized correctly, let go of the mouse button. The boulder will replace the circle outline.

Mountains, Embankments, and Ponds

Adding these scenic elements involves slightly different steps. To add these, perform the following steps:

1. Click on the Objects menu.

2. Click on the Scenery option.

3. Click on the 4 Level Mountain option.

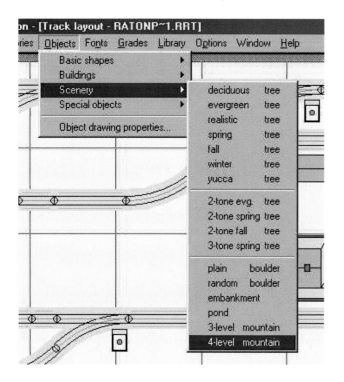

4. The mouse pointer will transform into a large plus with an x over it.

5. Move the mouse pointer to where the outer edge of the mountain will be.

6. Click your left mouse button.

7. The mouse pointer will transform into a white arrow with the word POINT under it.

8. Move the mouse pointer along the outer edge of the mountain, clicking periodically as you go to change the line direction. This will create a jagged line.

9. To complete the mountain, place your mouse pointer over the original point where the mountain started, and double-click.

10. The outline of the mountain will now fill in with various shades of brown color

Note: If the mountain covers the track, click on the Action menu and choose the Send To Back option.

Viewing the Layout Track List

Probably one of the most helpful features of the RR-Track Layout Design Software is its ability to automatically create a complete list of every M.T.H. RealTrax section and M.T.H. Accessory that you have placed on your track plan, along with quantity and prices. This makes it very easy when you go to your local hobby shop to get all the items you need to build your model railroad. To do this:

1. Click on the View menu.

2. Click on the Show Track List option.

Printing the Layout Track List

To print the Layout Track List, follow these steps:

1. Click on the Copy menu of the Layout Track List window.
2. Click on the Copy Contents to WRITE. WRITE is a very basic word processing program included with the Windows operating system.
3. The WRITE program will automatically launch a new document with the text of the layout items copied into it.
4. On the toolbar at the top of the WRITE window click on the Print button.

Note: You can also copy the contents of the Layout Track List and paste them into your favorite word processing program.

Other Topics

Among the many features of RR-Track Layout Design Software, there are several that I find very useful when creating track plans. These features will greatly enhance your track plan, and help make it easy to create them.

Adding Text Labels

In the process of creating your track plan, you may decide to place a town in a specific location. To place a text label to reference the name of the town, you can perform these steps:

1. Click on the Objects menu.
2. Click on the Special Objects option.
3. Click on the Text Label option.
4. In the Text Label dialog box, type the text you want to use for the label.

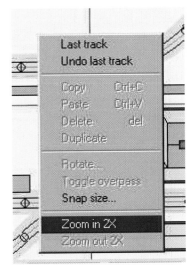

Note: Click on the Font button if you want to change size, typeface, or color of the text.

5. Click the OK button.
6. The mouse pointer will have a rectangle attached representing the text label. Move the mouse pointer to location where you want to place the text label.

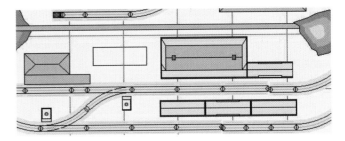

7. Click the mouse button.

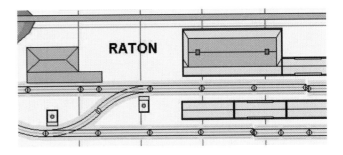

Zoom In and Zoom Out

Often you will find it useful to get a close-up view of an area of your track plan – much like using a magnifying glass. RR-Track Layout Design Software allows you to do this through the Zoom In and Zoom Out features.

Zoom In

To zoom in, perform the following steps:

1. In an open area of the track plan, click the right mouse button.
2. Click on the Zoom In 2X option.

3. The mouse pointer will transform into a rectangle with arrows inside, and the word ZOOM under it. It will have a larger outline rectangular box around it. Move the mouse to position the large rectangular outline box over the location that you want to zoom in on.

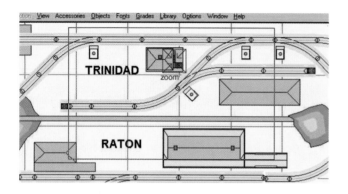

4. Click your left mouse button.

Note: You can continue to zoom in further by repeating the steps.

Zoom Out

To zoom out, perform these steps:

1. In an open area of the track plan, click the right mouse button.

2. Click on the Zoom Out 2X option.

Note: If you zoomed in several times in a row, you may need to zoom out several times in a row to get back to your original view size.

Relax Selected Track Configuration

As you place pieces of M.T.H. RealTrax on your track plan, you will come to the point of closing a loop as discussed earlier in this tutorial. When performing this task, more often than not you will find that although RR-Track Layout Design Software will close the loop, it will state that there is still a small gap between the two pieces of track and warn you about this fact. You need not be alarmed, as RR-Track Layout Design Software provides a great feature called Relax Selected Track Configuration. Though this is a more complex feature of the software, it is one of the most important in designing your track plan.

To begin, you must understand that although M.T.H. RealTrax has a rigid ABS plastic roadbed base attached, there is still a degree of flexibility in it – especially when more than one piece is involved. The Relax Selected Track Configuration allows you to take advantage of this flexibility in the software just as you would when putting the track together on your layout.

There are several important tips you should follow when using this feature. They are listed in the table below:

TIPS FOR USING THE RELAX SELECTED TRACK CONFIGURATION FEATURE

Tip	Description
Select pieces of track on both sides of the closure	You must do this otherwise the RR-Track Layout Design Software will not "know" that you want to close the gap.
Don't select too many pieces of track	Since RR-Track Layout Design Software iterates through movements of selected track, giving it too many pieces of track presents too many possibilities and will probably not produce desirable results.
Don't expect to make up a several-inch gap with this feature	If your gap is larger than an inch or two, I suggest trying to use a different track combination. One of the great benefits of M.T.H. RealTrax is that it was created using different sizes and curves, allowing you to mix and match to get the desired result that you need for your track plan.

To use the Relax Selected Track Configuration, follow these steps:

1. Click on a piece of track next to the gap you want to close. The selected track will turn red.

2. While holding the Shift key down, click on several consecutive pieces of track on both sides of the gap to select them. All of the selected track should be red.

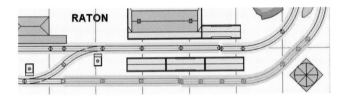

3. Click on the Action menu.

Note: If no track is selected, the Action menu will be grayed out and inaccessible.

4. Click on the Relax Selected Track Configuration option.

5. In the Selected Track Relaxation dialog box, click the x5 button once. The dialog will remain on the screen.

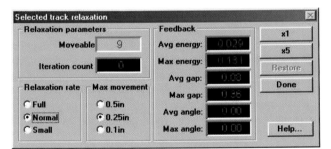

6. Look at your selected track to see if the move was enough. If the gap is still large, click on the x5 button again to continue closing the gap. When it gets close to closing, you can click on the x1 button.

Note: The x5 and x1 button represent the number of iterations the software will go through in performing the adjustment in the track in order to close the gap.

7. Once you are satisfied with how the track looks, click on the Done button in the Selected Track Relaxation dialog box.

Note: If you aren't satisfied with the result, click on the Restore button. This will undo the changes you made to the selected track and allow you start over

using either a different amount of selected track and/or a different sequence of the x5 and x1 buttons.

Printing Track Plans

Once you have completed your track plan and are satisfied with the results, you can easily print them in paper form. Having a paper copy of your finished track plan makes it easier when laying track during the construction process.

Changing Print Orientation

Depending on the track plan you design, you may want to change the orientation of the paper from portrait (up and down) to landscape (left and right) for the standard 8 1/2" by 11" paper. To do this, follow these steps:

1. Click on the File menu.

2. Click on the Printer option.

3. In the Printer dialog box, click on the Toggle button to change the paper orientation.

Note: Click the Toggle button again to change it back if you wish.

4. Click the OK button when finished.

Printing the Track Plan

To print your track plan, follow these steps:

1. Click on the File menu.

2. Click on the Print Layout option.

3. In the Print Layout dialog box, click on the Print button.

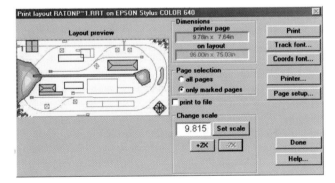

Changing the Scale for Printing

One terrific feature when printing your track plans in RR-Track Layout Design Software is the ability to change the print scale. Changing the print scale is like the zoom-in and zoom-out feature we saw earlier –

just that it is done on the paper. To work with this feature, you must first be in the Print Layout dialog box. To change the scale for printing, follow one of these two sets of steps:

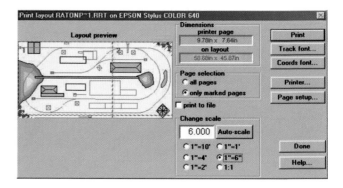

1. In the Change Scale area click on the +2x button. The Layout Preview on the left will show the updated scale with the red dashed lines representing the actual number of pieces of paper the layout will now be printed on.

2. To enlarge further, click on the +2x button again. To decrease the scale, click on the 2x button; or:

3. In the Change Scale area, click on the Set Scale button. This will change the options below it, allowing you to click on your choice of scales. For example: The 1 " = 1' choice would mean that one inch on the paper would equal one foot on the actual layout.

RR-Track Layout Design Software Reference

RR-Track Layout Design Software is a very extensive software application and contains many more features than are listed in this chapter. For more information on all features of RR-Track Layout Design Software, refer to either the Help system or the electronic Reference Manual included on the M.T.H. RailWare CD-ROM.

More Track Plans

Several track plans are included in Appendix 4, page 135.

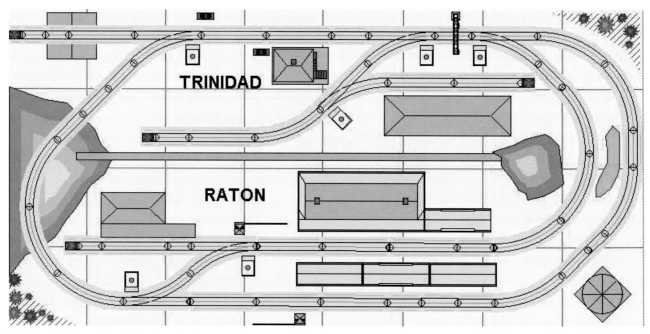

The Santa Fe Raton Pass Railroad track plan.

Constructing a Table for Your Model Railroad Layout

CHAPTER 5

By now, you are probably itching to start building something; you just want to get going! You've taken the time to think through your model railroad layout. You've done research to help in making it more realistic and have become more knowledgeable about your railroad. You've created a track plan using the RR-Track Layout Design Software included with the M.T.H. RailWare CD-ROM that will fit in the space available for your layout. You're ready to go.

It is at this point that we will take the ideas you have collected and turn them into a functional model train layout you can enjoy running your trains on for years to come. This chapter will deal with the first stage of construction – building a table for your train layout.

The big question as you start this phase of your train layout is where to get started. Once again, it is important take a few moments to think through this process before rushing into it. Poorly built train tables can cause a multitude of problems later.

As you begin, it is important to note a key term in building a train table. The term is "benchwork," and it refers to the construction and materials used in creating the foundation upon which your M.T.H. Electric Trains will run. For the rest of this chapter, when the term benchwork is used, it will refer to the physical construction and/or foundation of the train table.

What Type of Benchwork Should I Use?

One of the difficulties in building benchwork for a model train layout is that there are so many different methods to choose from. Entire books have been written on this subject alone, and if you ask several experienced modelers about this topic, you will hear just as many different ways to go about completing this task for your train layout.

In light of varied opinions, however, good benchwork construction shares several common factors. Using these factors, I will outline, describe, and construct the benchwork step by step for the Santa Fe Raton Pass Railroad.

If you have been involved in the model train hobby, you may have heard about a construction technique called "L-" girder benchwork. L-girder benchwork is a very good type of construction method, but many agree that it is a bit more complex, and so more experienced model railroaders use it. For the purposes of the Santa Fe Raton Pass Railroad, though, I will use a simpler approach, since we will be building a four by eight foot train layout table. This simpler method will provide a strong base for our M.T.H. Electric Trains layout along with a storage shelf below.

Do I Need a Carpenter?

A big fear of first time model train layout builders is whether they have the necessary skills to complete the benchwork. You don't need to be an expert carpenter to build a proper foundation for your layout. You do, however, need a few basic woodworking skills and tools to complete this phase of your layout. If you feel uncomfortable doing this, you may want to ask a friend who has experience in this area to help you out.

What Tools Do I Need?

Take a quick inventory of tools that you have around your house before you begin construction. Gather them together to avoid having to make several trips to the garage or tool shed to fetch them once you start. Compare what you have with the suggested list to see if you need to borrow or purchase the tools to complete the task. Many home improvement superstores now offer tool rentals at affordable prices.

LIST OF TOOLS

Item	Description
Safety glasses	Always be sure to wear safety glasses whenever working with tools.
Electric saw	Electric saws make precise, straight cuts of wood – circular or table saws work best.
Level	Using a level ensures that your construction is straight and level.
Adjustable wrench	An adjustable wrench is needed for the nuts and bolts that will hold the legs of the layout.
Screwdrivers	A cordless rechargeable screwdriver is a must-have.
Tape measure	Precise measurements will make construction easier.
Clamps – C or wood	Clamps hold pieces of wood together while connecting them.
Electric drill	Use an electric drill to make the holes for the screws and bolts.
Carpenter's square	Carpenter's squares give you perfect 90-degree angles on corners.
Pencil	Use a pencil to mark the wood for cuts and drilling holes.
Hammer	You'll need a hammer for a variety of purposes (but avoid using on thumbs).
Caulk gun	Use a caulk gun to apply Liquid Nails to the top of the benchwork.
File or wood rasp	A file gets the rough splinters off the wood after cutting and drilling.
Sandpaper	Smooth the edges of the wood with sandpaper for a nice finish.
Adhesive caulk	Liquid Nails for Projects works well and can be bought at most stores.

Making a Trip to Buy Building Supplies

The next step in the process of building the benchwork is to make a trip to the store to purchase the supplies necessary for construction. This can be done at a variety of places, including your local hardware store, lumberyard, or a home improvement superstore.

For the purposes of building the Santa Fe Raton Pass Railroad's benchwork, I have developed a detailed list of all the items needed for construction as shown below. You may want to take the list below with you when you go to purchase the supplies for your layout. When buying the bolts, nuts, and washers listed above, look for them in packages, as they are cheaper to buy in bulk than individually. You will end up with a few leftovers, but it will still probably cost you less money.

Homasote is a compressed paper fiber product that comes in four-by-eight-foot sheets. It is used in building construction for sound absorption, and will be used on the Santa Fe Raton Pass Railroad in the same capacity. I have found that some home improvement superstores do not carry this product, so you may need to get it at a regular lumberyard. This can be purchased later as it is the last item to be added to the benchwork in the process of construction. Additionally, if you are building a layout that requires cutting or sawing Homasote, you'll want to do that outside, as it will create a large amount of dust from the compressed paper fibers. Wear a respirator or mask to avoid inhaling the Homasote dust.

Looking down the length of a board makes it very easy to tell if it warped or not. If it is, keep searching until you find one that is straight.

BUILDING SUPPLIES

Quantity	Item
2 sheets	3/8" plywood, 4 ft. x 8 ft.
2	2" x 4"s – 8 ft. length
8	1" x 4"s – 8 ft. length
1 sheet	1/2" Homasote, 4 ft. x 8 ft.
1 box	1-5/8" black coarse dry wall screws
1 tube	Liquid Nails for Projects adhesive or similar product
16	1/4" diameter by 3-1/2" carriage bolts
16	1/4" nuts (wing or regular)
8	1/4" large diameter flat washers (a.k.a. fender washers)
1 sheet	1/4" Lauan plywood 4 ft. x 8 ft.

Inspecting the Wood Before Buying

It is important to carefully inspect each piece of wood before you buy it. Doing so will prevent you from purchasing defective and odd-shaped pieces of lumber that will be difficult or impossible to put together when you get home. Failure to do so may cause you to have to make another trip to the home improvement superstore or lumberyard. To avoid these problems, there are several tips you can keep in mind when inspecting wood.

The first tip when buying lumber is to remember that you get what you pay for. Spend a little more money for the higher-grade lumber; it is usually in better physical condition and it generally doesn't warp as bad as the cheaper grade. If you are unsure about the different grades of lumber, ask one of the store attendants to help you.

Another good tip for buying lumber is to check how wet the wood is. If it is wet or even damp, the wood will warp when it dries out – which can cause serious problems for your model railroad. Your best bet would be to try to buy wood that is (and has been) stored inside.

You'll generally have a wide range of plywood types and thicknesses from which to choose. For the Santa Fe Raton Pass Railroad, I chose 3/8" for the thickness, but if you want to go with extra thickness, that is perfectly fine. I would not recommend anything less than 3/8", as it wouldn't be sturdy enough for the top of the table.

Keep in mind that sheets of plywood usually have a rough side and a finished side; examine both sides before purchasing, and check all four corners to make sure they aren't damaged or defective. If you find a problem, simply put it back and continue searching for another sheet of plywood.

When selecting your 2x4s and 1x4s, avoid those that are damp or have an excessive amount of knots. One particularly good test is to take each board and hold it like a shotgun. Place the far end on the ground while you eye lengthwise down the board. This will allow you to see if the board is warped. If it is, put it back and look for another piece.

Let's Get Building

Before you begin construction, there are two very important facts to remember. First, when working with 1x4s and 2x4s, you need to know that these are not their actual measurements. A 1x4 in reality measures 3/4" by 3-1/2", while the 2x4 is really 1-1/2" by 3-1/2". Their true measurements will be of utmost importance as we measure and cut the wood needed to construct the various parts of the benchwork.

The second fact concerns taking measurements. Since we are human, we are prone to making mistakes, so always take measurements *twice* – even if you do so right after the first measurement – and always *before* cutting a piece of wood. This practice has saved me, on numerous occasions, from making a cut at the wrong spot. By measuring twice for each cut, you may avoid having to make an unnecessary trip back to the home improvement superstore or lumberyard.

The benchwork for your layout will be done in four stages. These stages are: **Base, Leg Supports, Storage Shelf Area,** and **Table Top**. I will take you through each step, one at a time, and provide detailed instructions and photographs on how to accomplish them.

Constructing the Base

Let's begin by putting those safety glasses on, and, as always, when working with any power tools, be careful to use them properly to avoid injury. Keep in mind that this part of the construction will create quite a bit of sawdust, so you may want to work outside or in the garage.

The first stage of the benchwork deals with the train table base. The base will be made up of 1x4s and will be configured in a four-by-eight-foot rectangle frame.

To start, lay two eight-foot long 1x4s down parallel to each other, about four feet apart. It is a good idea to measure both pieces just to make sure that they are eight feet long. Next, cut two of the 1x4s to make the end pieces. Since the short end of the frame will need to measure four feet exactly when pieced together, it is very important to factor in the width of the two long-sided 1x4s. Therefore, each of the short 1x4s will need to be cut to a length of 46-1/2" (3/4" + 3/4" + 46-1/2" = 48").

Once you have completed cutting the 1x4s, use the file to remove the rough edges. You may also want to use a little sandpaper to make the ends smooth before you piece the 1x4s together.

Take the cut 1x4s and lay them at each end so that they can be fastened together to make the frame. Place the carpenter's square outside the first corner you choose to fasten together. Though nails can be used, I recommend using screws because they are much more secure, and won't loosen over time. Since 1x4s are made of pine or white wood, they are relatively soft, so you don't necessarily need to drill a pilot hole for each screw. If you feel more comfortable drilling small pilot holes, go ahead and do so. Space the screws apart so that there will be room for three of them for each corner connecting the 1x4s together. One good idea here is to only put one screw in per corner about half way. This will allow you to adjust the base as you finish putting in the other screws.

At this point, your rectangular frame base is put together. Don't worry if it doesn't seem very stable, as the crossbeam 1x4s you will put in next will help cure

A 1x4 is not truly 1" by 4", so be sure to take this into account when taking measurements for train layout.

this problem. To begin putting these crossbeams in place, take your pencil and mark the eight-foot side of your frame base every two feet. You should make three marks on the wood, and will want to repeat this process on the other eight-foot side of your frame base.

Next, cut three more 1x4s to a length of 46-1/2" (this is the same length as the ends of the frame): these will be our crossbeams. Once you are finished cutting them, use your file to remove any rough edges. Place each crossbeam, upright, inside the frame approximately where each of the marks we made on the outside of the frame are. Making sure to line up the first crossbeam, put one screw in about half way. Go to the other side of the crossbeam and do the same. It is very important that the crossbeam does not stick up above the top of the outside frame that you are connecting it to, because the plywood top will eventually be placed on top of this. If it is uneven, it will be difficult to attach the plywood to the frame.

The 1x4s are laid out and ready to be fastened together. This frame is what the plywood will be mounted upon.

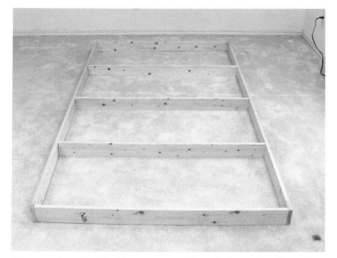

The crossbeams will add support not only to the base, but also to the plywood top when it is applied later on.

Once you are satisfied with the crossbeam placement, finish putting the screw all the way in, and add two more screws to make the crossbeam more secure. Repeat these steps for each of the other two crossbeams. When you are finished, you will have a sturdy base to which we will attach the leg supports.

Leg Supports

Now that the construction of the base is complete, it is time to put legs on the benchwork. For this, we will use 2x4s, as they will provide additional strength to support the base compared to the smaller 1x4s.

At this point, you will have to decide how high you want your train table to be. Pick a height you like best, although the general idea is to choose somewhere between 24" and 48". Anything lower or higher will have certain disadvantages. For the Santa Fe Raton Pass Railroad I chose 36" as the length of the legs – a height that will allow me to easily work on the layout and reach items toward the middle of the table. Also, most children will still be able to see the trains while they run on the layout. Just be sure to measure and mark the wood before making any cuts. These cuts should be as straight as possible. If you accidentally have an angle on the cut, it may cause your table to be a little unstable when complete. Once you are finished cutting the 2x4s, file and sand the edges to get rid of any splinters before the next step.

You are now ready to connect the 2x4 legs to the base of the train table. For this step, use the 3-1/2" carriage bolts with wing nuts and washers. Using bolts will allow you to easily take the legs off later in case you need to move or store the layout.

Since we will connect the legs on the inside of the 1x4 base, you will need to use your pencil to mark on the outer side of the base in much the same way as

Don't worry about legs being upright – you will flip the table over so the legs rest on the floor once all of them are installed.

when you put the crossbeams in place. Use the tape measure to locate a place 12" from each corner on the long sides of the base, and mark; you'll use this to align the legs in order to drill the holes for the bolts. Next, place the first leg upright inside the base aligned with the mark you just made – making sure it is flush with the bottom of the base. If you are putting your table together on carpet, you may want to put a scrap piece of plywood or cardboard underneath it to help keep it flush. Don't worry about the legs facing upward at this point, as you will simply flip the base and legs right side up when the legs are all fastened.

Before drilling the holes, take a C-clamp, and tighten it to hold the leg and base together. Use a level to make sure the 2x4 leg is upright. Once you have it correct, tighten the C-clamp fully. Now, using your electric drill, make two holes diagonally from one another through the base and leg, being careful to avoid hitting the C-clamp when drilling the holes.

Once you are done making the holes, slide the bolts through, using washers on the nut ends of the bolt (they help keep the wood from being damaged when you tighten them). Next, gently tighten the nuts on the bolts, but don't make them very tight just yet. Use your level to check the upright leg on two consecutive sides to ensure that the leg is not set on an angle. Even though we checked this before, sometimes the vibration from the drilling can cause it to move. If it is not level, you can gently nudge the leg with your hand to make it straight. When you are satisfied, tighten the nuts on the bolts securely to keep the leg in the correct position. It is a good idea to check the leg with the level again after you tighten the nuts on the bolts. Repeat this process for each of the other three legs.

The last step involves flipping the base of the table over so that the ends of the legs rest on the floor. You will need two people to perform this task. With one person at each of the short ends of the base, carefully lift the base and rotate it, being sure not to put pressure on the sides of the legs as you do this. Continue rotating the base until you can set all four legs down squarely on the floor.

Storage Shelf Area

The third stage in building the benchwork for the train table involves making the storage shelf area below the base. This area will serve several important functions. First, it will provide added strength and stability to the train table, as it connects the four legs together. Secondly, the storage shelf will provide a nice area to store the boxes that your M.T.H. Electric Trains and accessories come in. Lastly, with the new Digital Command System (DCS), you can use the storage shelf to hold your M.T.H. Z-4000 Transformer, as well

as other components for the layout.

The first step in this phase involves deciding how high off the ground you want the storage shelf. For the Santa Fe Raton Pass Railroad, I chose a height of 6", as it would allow for easy access underneath as well as additional storage space. Move this measurement up or down according to your needs.

The storage shelf area will be built in largely the same fashion as the base that you previously put together in that you will utilize 1x4s for its construction. To begin, cut two 1x4s down to six-foot lengths. Again, be sure to file off any rough edges from the cuts. Using the tape measure and a pencil, make a mark 6" up from the floor on each leg. With two C-clamps, take the first six-foot long 1x4, and clamp it in place with the bottom of the 1x4, lining up where the 6" mark is. Once this is done, use your level to make sure that the 1x4 is not at an angle.

If it is, loosen the C-clamp to make the adjustments needed and then retighten the C-clamp.

You are then ready drill two holes in diagonal manner (just like when you connected the legs to the base) for the bolts to fit through. When complete,

Use a level to make sure the 1x4 for the storage shelf area is level before attaching it to the legs of the train table.

It is also a good idea to make sure the legs are level.

With the C-clamp still tightened, slide the carriage bolts in place with washers, and fasten the wing nuts in place.

Slide the piece of plywood for the storage shelf into place.

slide the bolts through with the washers in place and screw the nuts on tight. Repeat this process for the other side of the train table.

The next step will be to put three crossbeams in place to connect the two six-foot-long 1x4s you bolted to the legs; cut them to a length of 46-1/2". Before putting the crossbeams in place, mark both of the bolted six-foot 1x4s with a pencil at the one-, three-, and five-foot intervals. Connect one crossbeam at a time, lining them up with their respective pencil marks. Since they are not lying on the ground, it is very helpful if you can have another person hold them while you put the screws in place. You will probably want to put two or three screws in the ends of each crossbeam. Repeat this process for the other two crossbeams.

Cut one of the sheets of plywood so that it measures 64" by 46". Then, simply take this piece and lay it over the three crossbeams you just screwed into place.

Carefully line up the piece of plywood so that the long edges are flush with the outside 1x4s that you bolted to the legs. Once it is lined up, use screws to fasten it to the 1x4s.

At each corner, place four more screws evenly along the outer 1x4s.

Next, take a piece of 1x4 or 2x4 that is preferably four-feet long, and line it up with the screws that hold each of the crossbeams in place. Use a pencil to draw a line across the plywood shelf. This line will guide you in placing two, evenly spaced screws through the plywood and into the crossbeam.

You may notice that the table still doesn't seem very sturdy at this point. But don't worry – we're not done yet with this step. Take the leftover piece of plywood (30" by 48") that you made the storage shelf

from, and cut it in half lengthwise, so that each piece measures 15" by 48". Fasten each of these, lengthwise, from leg-to-leg as shown in fig. 13.

In addition to making the table sturdy, they will

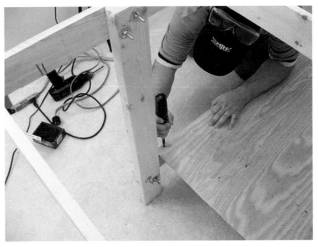

The use of an electrical screw driver makes screwing the storage shelf in place much easier.

To provide more support for the train table, use the extra plywood to make a component-mounting wall for the Digital Command System (DCS); attach the wall to the legs.

To avoid excessive splintering, clamp a piece of scrap wood on the back side of the crossbeam as you drill.

also serve another purpose as well. Later, we will mount the Digital Command System (DCS) components on one of these pieces in order to make wiring easier and conserve space on the storage shelf. From now on, we will refer to these pieces of plywood as component mounting walls.

The last step in creating the storage shelf is to prepare it for the electrical wiring that will be needed when you set up the track and accessories for the Digital Command System (DCS). This will involve drilling several large holes in each of the crossbeams of the base for the wiring from various points of the layout to the component-mounting wall. Using a 1" spade drill-bit, place three holes in each of the crossbeams.

It is not necessary to measure for the placement of these holes, but you'll want them to spread out relatively evenly. One very good trick is to use two C-clamps to temporarily place a piece of scrap wood on the backside of the crossbeam as you drill.

This will keep the back side of the crossbeam from splintering too much. When you complete drilling these holes, file any rough edges off.

Table Top

The last of the four stages in creating a train table is the quickest and easiest one of all. Take the remaining piece of plywood and place it on top of the base.

Carefully align the edges so that they are flush with the 1x4 sides of the base. Use screws to fasten the plywood to the base around the outer edges so that the screws go into the 1x4s.

Place them roughly every 12" to 18" apart. Like the storage shelf below, place several screws in each of the crossbeams. Again, take a piece of wood and mark a line across the plywood where each of the crossbeams are, and then simply put the screws in place. I suggest placing three screws in each crossbeam, being careful not to put one where we drilled the 1" holes in the crossbeam for wiring.

The last step is to place the 4x8 sheet of Homasote directly on top of the plywood.

At this point, you may be asking yourself if this is really necessary. You may be rationalizing that Homasote is an extra cost and that the plywood is good enough and the Homasote isn't necessary. But

A 1" spade drill bit works best for making wiring holes through the crossbeams.

Slide the 4x8 sheet of plywood on to the top of the base.

Align the plywood with the edges and insert screws into the 1x4s underneath.

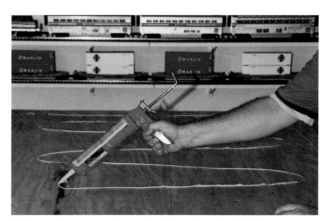

Use a caulk gun to apply an adhesive such as Liquid Nails for Projects directly on the plywood before attaching the Homasote on top.

Homasote is a sound-absorbing, compressed paper product that is very important to your model railroad, due to the "speaker effect" of plywood. To illustrate the speaker effect, I have a friend who built a train layout several years ago and decided not to use Homasote. Instead, he saved a few dollars by screwing his track directly to the plywood. He discovered that the vibration from his trains going over the tracks transmitted through the screws to the underside of the plywood, and amplified the sound. His very noisy layout made it difficult to hear the sounds from his M.T.H. engines over the vibration sounds. Placing Homasote on top of your plywood will help prevent the speaker effect from happening.

Use your caulk gun to liberally apply the Liquid Nails for Projects (or other similar adhesive) all over the plywood.

Next, place the sheet of Homasote right on top of it, making sure that the edges are flush with the edges of the plywood. You'll have several minutes to move it around as the Liquid Nails takes 10 minutes to set. When it is positioned correctly, place several screws through the Homasote into the plywood; they temporarily help to hold the Homasote closely to the plywood while the Liquid Nails adhesive dries and bonds to the plywood. Leave the screws in place overnight before removing them.

Your train table is now complete and you have a sturdy, well-built foundation for your M.T.H. Electric Trains to run on. The time and effort you have taken will pay dividends of enjoyment down the road as you move on to the next aspect of building your realistic model railroad.

Insert screws into the Homasote to help the Liquid Nails bond it to the plywood. Once dry, remove the screws to avoid the "speaker effect."

This cross section shows the Homasote on the top, followed by the plywood and the 1x4 base.

CHAPTER 6

Track Laying and Backdrop Construction

Backdrops like the one the Santa Fe Raton Pass Railroad dramatically improve the realism of model railroad layouts.

The research and planning are done, and you have spent some time creating your track plan. The train table is built. You are now ready to start laying your M.T.H. RealTrax. It is at this point that your layout will really begin to take shape and come to life, and all of the prior labor begins to pay off.

This chapter will focus on track laying, and placing buildings and accessories on the Santa Fe Raton Pass Railroad. We'll follow the track plan created using the RR-Track Layout Design Software discussed in Chapter 4. We will also install a scenic divider equipped with a realistic backdrop. This backdrop will help to make the layout appear larger than it really is, and provide a basis for the construction of the realistic scenery.

Painting the Table Top

Before a single piece of track is put in place, it's a good idea to paint the Homasote table top to provide a base color for the application of the scenery later. I suggest using a medium- to light-brown or tan color, avoiding dark brown, since most of the Homasote will eventually be covered with track, buildings, roads, and ground cover. You can save some money by purchasing cans of incorrectly mixed paint at your local home improvement or hardware store. More often than not, you can purchase a gallon of this paint for just a few dollars. For the Santa Fe Raton Pass Railroad, I was able to find a gallon of tan paint for only $3.

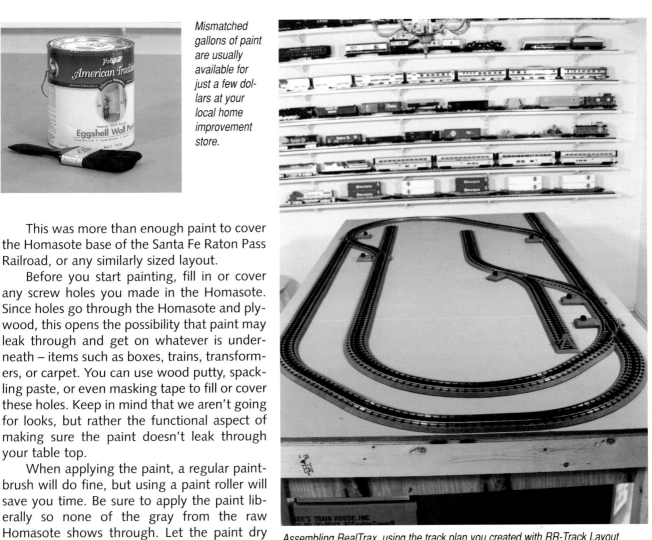

This was more than enough paint to cover the Homasote base of the Santa Fe Raton Pass Railroad, or any similarly sized layout.

Before you start painting, fill in or cover any screw holes you made in the Homasote. Since holes go through the Homasote and plywood, this opens the possibility that paint may leak through and get on whatever is underneath – items such as boxes, trains, transformers, or carpet. You can use wood putty, spackling paste, or even masking tape to fill or cover these holes. Keep in mind that we aren't going for looks, but rather the functional aspect of making sure the paint doesn't leak through your table top.

When applying the paint, a regular paintbrush will do fine, but using a paint roller will save you time. Be sure to apply the paint liberally so none of the gray from the raw Homasote shows through. Let the paint dry for at least a day before continuing to the next step.

Assembling RealTrax, using the track plan you created with RR-Track Layout Design Software, is a breeze.

When putting the track together, use an abrasive pad to remove the blackened top from the center rail of the RealTrax. Removing this coating provides better electrical conductivity and improved performance of your M.T.H. Electric Trains.

Laying M.T.H. RealTrax

This is an important step: Although it will wear off over a period of prolonged use, to prevent the black coating of the center rail from impeding normal electrical conductivity, you'll need to remove it. To remove the coating, use an abrasive pad such as a Brite-Boy scouring pad, a track-cleaning eraser of the type sold at most hobby shops, or even very fine-grit sandpaper. Buff the center rail's flat top surface until the silver of the rail is showing. Follow this by gently rubbing a damp cloth

A RailKing Y6b Locomotive clears the station platforms coming out of the turn at Raton.

over the rails to pick up any small particles rubbed off the center rail or the abrasive pad.

Now, using a printout of the track plan that you created with the *RR-Track Layout Design Software*, take your M.T.H. RealTrax sections and begin to assemble your trackwork on the train table. Since you spent time earlier creating and refining your track plan, this process should go rather quickly. I was able to put the Santa Fe Raton Pass Railroad track together in roughly 15 minutes.

I think you will find the experience very satisfying as you watch the plan on paper become a reality on your train table. Don't screw the track down yet, though; you'll screw the track down securely once everything is working according to plan and fits properly. What you're doing now is simply a preliminary "test" setup of the track.

At this point, you'll start to gain an appreciation for the very realistic appearance of M.T.H. RelaTrax. Not only are the sections easy to fit together, but the molded gray roadbed, black ties, and blackened center rail provide a great visual improvement over the tubular type of track that had been standard in the O gauge hobby for so long.

Placing Buildings and Accessories

The next step is to place buildings and accessories in their respective locations on the layout. Suddenly, you will see how your railroad empire is rapidly taking shape! You planned for the location of each item on paper, but now you'll see them in a three-dimensional world, and things will look a bit different.

Be flexible at this point. Don't hesitate to switch

things around to your heart's content. It's *your* layout and you can certainly change your mind. On the Santa Fe Raton Pass Railroad, I did just that. Originally, I had a siding planned for Raton, where the M.T.H. Operating O Scale Water Tower (Item 30-11028) now sits. I felt that siding was too small and that the water tower would be better suited to that location, so I just eliminated the siding altogether. Another change I made involved a small building I had planned to have right next to the M.T.H. Operating Coaling Tower (Item 30-9043). In setting these accessories on the table, I thought the building looked too small sitting next to the large Coaling Tower, so I decided to use that space to make the planned mountain a little larger.

When placing buildings and accessories, be sure to include various track signals, such as the O Scale Operating Semaphore (Item 30-11023) and Cantilevered Signal Bridge (Item 30-11009). These devices are activated by M.T.H.'s Infrared Track Activation Device (or ITAD), so you will want to be sure to place the ITADs in their proper operating positions as well. On the Santa Fe Raton Pass Railroad, I chose to use the more realistic looking M.T.H. O Scale ITAD Signal Box (Item 30-1028) that resembles a trackside electrical box, rather than the regular M.T.H. RealTrax ITADs (Item 40-1028).

If you find it necessary to make significant changes, you may want to consider going back and revising your track plan using the RR-Track *Layout Design Software* on your computer. There are several advantages to doing this, such as assuring that the changes will fit in the given space, and obtaining an exact count of the different sections of RealTrax need-

Area	Details
Tunnel Portals and Interiors	Set the tunnel portals in the location where you want them to be. Make sure the tunnel's interior has plenty of room on both sides of the track, and that all locomotives and cars clear the sides without scraping. Also, allow for some sort of access to the tunnel – derailments inside of tunnels are not fun to deal with.
Bridges	A good guideline for vertical clearance is 7" from the top of the track to bottom of bridge.
Curved Track Sections	Trains need more side-to-side clearance on curves, so be sure to account for this.
Parallel Tracks	Be sure the tracks aren't spaced too closely (especially going into and out of curved tracks), as overhang from one train may sideswipe another.

ed for the change – important considerations that will save you money and extra trips to the hobby shop.

Checking Train Clearances

Once you are satisfied with the location of your buildings and accessories, you will need to temporarily connect your Z-4000 Transformer to the track so you can perform a test run to check the clearance of your trains as they travel around the layout. It would certainly be an unpleasant surprise to build your whole layout, only to discover that your favorite passenger cars don't fit through a tunnel, or that your favorite big steam engine scrapes against the water tower every time it passes by. In the planning phase done earlier, it isn't always easy to tell if structures or accessories are too close to the track, so a test run is a "must do" before moving on and attaching these items permanently to your layout. Besides, running your M.T.H. Electric Trains is so much fun that you can regard this as an early reward for all the effort you have put into your model railroad empire to this point.

For the Santa Fe Raton Pass Railroad, I used just one track lock-on to test run the trains because the Z-4000 transformer could easily handle the task for a layout of this size. Don't worry about the Digital Command System (DCS) components just yet, as their installation and use will be covered in a later chapter.

A good rule of thumb to follow when initially running trains on a new layout, or on a new section of an existing layout, is to check for clearance by using the biggest and/or largest engines and rolling stock that you have. It is extremely important that the first time you run your engines and cars around your railroad that you do it *very slowly*. You may even want to get

a friend or family member to help you do this, so that one person can stay at the transformer and the other can walk around the layout with the train to check the clearances. Several areas on a typical layout require special attention to clearances, and these are described on the list above:

Problems and Solutions on the Santa Fe Raton Pass Railroad

On the Santa Fe Raton Pass Railroad I ran into two problems in the area of clearance, both of which involved the Single Tunnel Portals. The first problem related to height clearance with a RailKing Intermodel Stack Car. I placed the tunnel portals in the location

A 1" block of foam was added under the tunnel portals to help with vertical clearance of the intermodal stack cars.

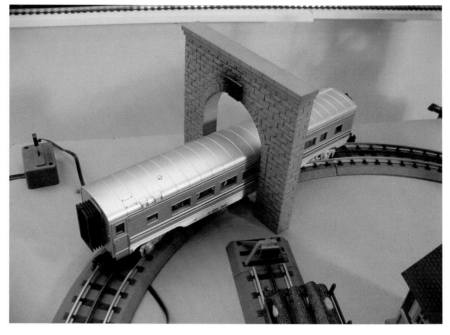

I used a RailKing Santa Fe 60' Streamlined passenger car to check the side overhand clearance on the tunnel portal.

they would occupy when the mountain was ultimately constructed. However, the top of the Intermodel Stack Car kept knocking the tunnel portals over. To remedy this, I placed a small, one-inch-tall block of Woodland Scenics Foam under each side of the tunnel portal to give it some additional elevation.

The second problem encountered on the Santa Fe Raton Pass Railroad involved the sideways clearance of the tunnel portal in the town of Raton. This particular portal was placed on a curve, and when I ran my larger engines and cars, their overhang on both the inside and outside of the curve would not allow them to make it through. Fixing this problem took a little more work. I cut the tunnel portal in half vertically at the top of the arch as shown.

I then cut a 1" section out of an extra tunnel portal and glued this piece between the two halves of the original tunnel. This created a wider portal, which allowed the largest trains to pass through without scraping the sides.

Since the double portal would have been too large, I cut a single in half, and added a small section between to make it wider.

Use a piece of wood on the back side to help in aligning the pieces when you glue them together.

Outlining Buildings and Accessories

Once you are satisfied with the placement of all the buildings and accessories, take a pencil and outline around the base of each item.

Write the name or an abbreviation in each area to provide you a quick reference later on, since the structures will be temporarily removed from the layout.

Use the pencil to outline the track since it isn't permanently affixed to the table at this point. This is important because a sudden accidental movement of the track will necessitate redoing the clearance testing conducted earlier.

If you choose to have mountains or streams like the Santa Fe Raton Pass Railroad, then you will also need to outline the placement of these items to help when you build them later on. Mark the exact position of any tunnel portals and dividers if you are using these items on your layout.

Be sure to outline all the building structures, and then remove them from the layout to keep them from getting damaged when creating the scenery.

Write the name of each building or accessory inside the outlined area for reference later on.

Pre-Wiring

As a prelude to the next step, remove all buildings and accessories from the train table. It is best to have them out of the way to avoid possible damage as you work on the wiring and installation of the divider. For that matter, you should also keep the table clear of structures and other accessories while you're creating your scenery – a topic covered in the next chapter.

Using an electric drill with a 1/4" bit, carefully drill holes through the tabletop for the wires that will be used to light buildings and activate accessories (remember to wear your safety glasses). For most of the buildings, you will probably want to place this hole in the middle of the pencil outline made for that item. For accessories such as the Operating Crossing Gates or Cantilevered Signal Bridge, however, you should drill the hole right next to the outline since the wires for these accessories usually come out from the sides of their bases. It's a good idea to keep the actual accessory handy so that you can refer to it to see exactly where its wires or connecting terminals are located.

After you drill each hole, get underneath the layout and use a pencil to write the name of the accessory next to the hole.

This will make it much easier to run the final connections of wires to the Digital Command System (DCS) – a procedure covered later in this book.

Several additional holes will need to be drilled for the wires that feed power to the track. Whenever you are building a layout, it's a good idea to run several "feeder" wires to various locations around your layout. This procedure will assure a more even distribution of power to all sections of the layout, since some amount of current is lost as it travels through rail joints and the track itself.

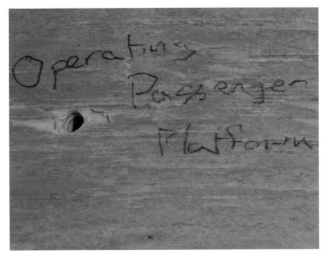

Label all the holes you drill for wiring under the layout table. This will make it much easier when hooking up the wires later on.

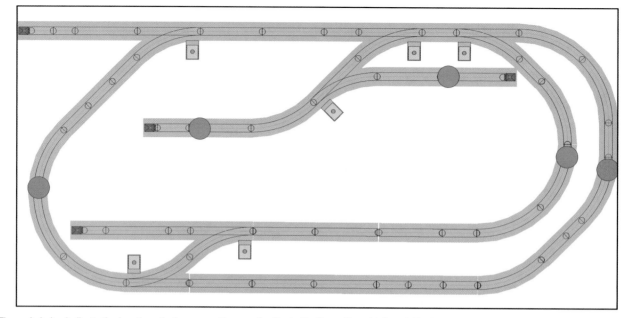

The red circles indicate the location of wire connections on the Santa Fe Raton Pass Railroad. For better electrical conductivity, connect several "feeder" wires to provide even power around your layout.

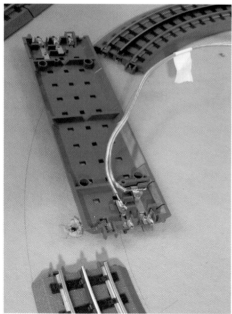

Connecting the wires on the bottom of the RealTrax allows you to completely hide the wire connections.

Use solder to connect the wires to the metal connectors underneath the RealTrax sections.

It is also very important that you use a specific kind of wire for your track power connections. M.T.H. recommends 16-gauge twisted pair (stereo speaker) wire for use with the Digital Command System (DCS).

If you choose to use a standard RealTrax Power Lockon, place the holes right next to each of the connecting posts. For the Santa Fe Raton Pass Railroad, however, I chose to solder the wires directly to the bottom of the RealTrax sections. This is a bit more work, as well as being slightly more difficult, but I felt that the RealTrax Power Lockon wasn't very realistic in appearance. By soldering power wires directly to the track, I was able to drill holes for the wiring right where the RealTrax lay, thereby effectively masking both the wires and the connecting points, which were hidden under the plastic molded-on roadbed of the RealTrax.

In making the track power connections, I cut 10" lengths of the 16-gauge twisted pair wire and soldered them to the metal connectors on the bottom of the RealTrax, as shown in fig. 17. The 10" wires provide enough length to fit through the hole to the underside of the layout, where they will eventually be connected to the Digital Command System (DCS).

Using a Scenic Divider and Backdrop

When I planned the Santa Fe Raton Pass Railroad, one primary feature I wanted was realistic operation. To help achieve this goal, I devised a track plan that featured two towns: Raton, New Mexico, and Trinidad, Colorado. With the limited space of a four-by-eight foot layout, I had to employ a scenic divider lengthwise across the layout to give the appearance of two geographically separated locations.

A divider is simply a board placed upright to physically divide two areas on a layout. It's a great device for the model railroader as it serves several purposes: First, it distinguishes two areas for the trains to travel to and from. Second, a divider creates an illusion for the observer by making the layout seem larger than it really is – allowing trains to disappear and reappear from one town or area to the next. Third, and probably most important, the application of a high-quality backdrop to both flat surfaces of the divider will dramatically increase the realism of your model railroad.

Constructing the Divider

To create a scenic divider for your layout, choose a sturdy, thin board, such as Masonite or Lauan, in 1/4" thickness. If you choose Masonite, I suggest getting the tempered type, as it is quite a bit sturdier than the regular kind. This is important because the divider will stand upright on your layout without a whole lot of vertical support, so the sturdier it is, the better. Both types of board are sold in four-by-eight-foot sheets, and can be purchased at most home improvement stores or lumber yards. I chose to use Lauan for the divider used on the Santa Fe Raton Pass Railroad.

The overall dimensions of your divider will depend on several factors. First, the kind of backdrop you purchase will determine the height of the divider. For the Santa Fe Raton Pass Railroad, I used two of the excellent backdrops available from BackDrop Warehouse (see sidebar), and was able to pick my height of 18". You will also need to determine the proper length for your divider. Again, this will depend on the backdrop you use, as well as how you plan to transition the backdrop to your layout. I chose a length of five feet for the Santa Fe Raton Pass Railroad. Though it can be used effectively in certain situations, I would not recommend simply placing a board upright down the middle of your layout. Instead, try to use transition items, such as mountains or buildings, at the ends of the divider in order to avoid a sudden "drop-off" at either end. The Santa Fe Raton Pass Railroad makes use of mountains at both ends. As you can see, this produces a nice effect. Additionally, these mountains help to add support to the divider.

Applying the Backdrop

Once you have determined the size of divider needed, you can cut your board to size, being sure to file and sand any rough edges. Save the excess pieces of board; you can use them later for a variety of things. If possible, use a table saw for cutting the divider board since this is the easiest way to get perfectly straight cuts. If you don't have a table saw, perhaps a friend or neighbor can help you out. I cut the Santa Fe Raton Pass Railroad's divider to a length of 60" and a height of 18".

When the divider is cut to size, check your backdrops for proper fit by laying them on the divider board. Since the 18" tall backdrops from BackDrop Warehouse came in eight-foot lengths, I trimmed them to the correct length to fit on the divider. I did this by measuring; marking a line with a pencil and straight edge; and then cutting the background with a pair of scissors. I saved the excess sections of the backdrop, since they also will be used later on.

Now, it's time to apply your backdrop to both sides of the divider. The backdrops from BackDrop Warehouse come with directions that detail several methods to accomplish this (they also provide the directions on their Web site, as well). For the Santa Fe Raton Pass Railroad, I used double-sided carpet tape, which is inexpensive and can be purchased at most home improvement stores. Carpet tape works well because it is very thin and extremely tacky.

I started by applying tape along the outer edge of the divider, leaving about 1/4" space between it and the edge. I followed this by placing tape across the length of the divider about halfway down.

Since the carpet tape has peel-off backing on one side, I left the backing on while placing the tape on the divider. Once all the tape was in place on the divider, I peeled off the backing. I then placed the rolled-up backdrop on one side of the divider and slowly unrolled it, lengthwise, pressing down firmly as I went along. It is extremely important to unroll the backdrop slowly, making sure that the edges stay in line with the edges of the divider.

If you do make a mistake, very slowly and carefully peel the backdrop off the tape to prevent it from tearing. Repeat this process to connect the second background to the other side of the divider.

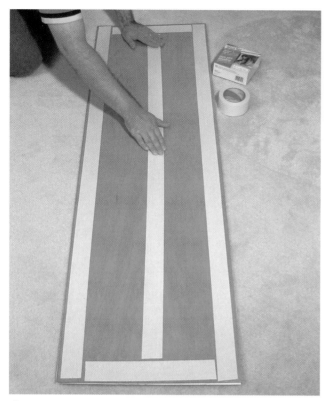

Because carpet tape is thin and very tacky, it's an excellent adhesive for mounting the backdrop onto the divider.

Peel off the carpet tape backing when you are ready to mount the backdrop.

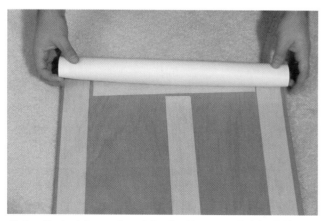

Roll up the backdrop and carefully align it at one end of the divider.

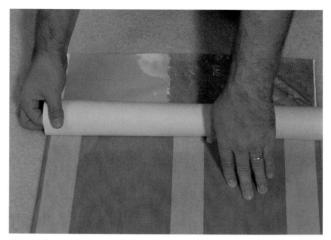

Unroll the backdrop slowly, making sure to keep it lined up with the edges. Press down firmly to help it adhere to the carpet tape underneath.

Attach the "L" brackets to the divider first and then attach them to train table making sure to align them with the pencil marks you made earlier.

Installing the Divider

With the backdrops in place, you are now ready to install the divider. Attach two 3" "L" brackets to the divider before you install the divider on the train table. Using 1" screws, attach the brackets in place at the base of the divider near each end. Don't worry about the way they look, because scenic items will eventually cover the brackets.

After the brackets are attached to the divider, place the divider upright on the train table, carefully fitting it in the location that you marked earlier with your pencil. When you are satisfied with its position, attach the other leg of the "L" brackets to the train table.

You may want to get a friend or family member to hold the divider as you perform this task.

A divider with a backdrop provides an immediate impact by making a small layout seem much larger. In the next chapter, we'll work on increasing that impact with the construction of realistic scenery.

Creating Realistic Scenery

Real life is not flat. Your layout shouldn't be flat, either. Just look around you – even some of the "flattest" areas still have slight dips and changes in elevation as well as occasional large rocks that protrude out of the area around them. The next phase in building your model railroad layout with M.T.H. Electric Trains involves putting the "realistic" in the phrase "realistic model railroading" by constructing mountains and streams, trees, grass, roads, and rocks. The proper addition and use of scenery on your model railroad will greatly add to the realism, credibility, and believability of your layout. And in many cases, it can be used to make your model railroad layout seem larger than it actually is.

For many model railroaders, construction of scenery is a scary topic largely due to their fear of making mistakes. Some model railroaders rush without

a plan into this phase of building a layout, and the results are not very attractive. Others simply add as little scenery as possible to avoid this phase altogether. For the sake of realism, don't rush *or* avoid this part of your layout! Instead, let me assure you that anyone can create realistic scenery with a little time and effort.

Woodland Scenics

All of the scenery on the Santa Fe Raton Pass Railroad was constructed using Woodland Scenics products (see sidebar at the end of this chapter). They provide a full line of products that are easy to use and generate strikingly realistic results. The rest of this chapter will focus on the steps necessary to use the excellent products from Woodland Scenics to build realistic scenery in order to transform your flat train table into a very authentic replica of a real life railroad.

In addition to these products, Woodland Scenics offers a complete line for the model railroader. Their products are so easy to use that even a person with no experience can produce fantastic results.

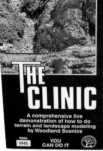

Before you begin, I recommend that you obtain two items from Woodland Scenics that will not end up on your layout, but are every bit as important as those that do: "The Clinic" video and the *Woodland Scenics Scenery Manual*. "The Clinic" video is a step-by-step demonstration of how to use Woodland Scenics products to produce realistic scenery. If you are concerned about your ability to create scenery, then this video is an absolute must for you. I found it very valuable since I was able to see the steps and techniques involved on the video before I repeated them in the Santa Fe Raton Pass Railroad. In watching "The Clinic," I also found that it gave me confidence by showing that the construction is relatively easy to do.

The *Woodland Scenics Scenery Manual* is a book that contains fully detailed, yet simple "How To" instructions, along with proven advice and insider tips for achieving terrific results on your model railroad. It also contains valuable step-by-step pictures using Woodland Scenics products. This book is a must-have scenery construction reference for the model railroader.

Woodland Scenics

Woodland Scenics is recognized by many model railroading enthusiasts as a leading provider of realistic scenery and terrain materials. Based in Linn Creek, Missouri, Woodland Scenics has been in business since 1975 producing top-notch products, helping hobbyists to produce extremely realistic scenery on their model railroad layouts. Over the course of time, this focus on serving the needs of model railroaders has helped Woodland Scenics become the largest maker of model railroad scenery in the world.

To demonstrate how easy their products are to use, Woodland Scenics once gave an eleven year old a scenery kit to build. The eleven year old had no trouble using the kit to produce fine looking scenery. So, if an eleven year old can do it, you can, too!

Woodland Scenics carries a complete line of products, from trees to rock molds to Realistic Water to ground cover – whatever the model railroader needs, they have it. To view their wide-ranging product line, visit their Web site at: www.woodlandscenics.com, or your local hobby shop.

The addition of a border using 1/4" Lauan gives your layout a finished look, as well providing a base for scenery to be built up against.

Layout Border Siding

The first step in the construction of scenery on your layout involves creating a border around the entire outer edges of the train table. This border will serve several important functions. First, it will vary in height according to the elevation level of the terrain. This provides a strong base to support scenic elements such as mountains. Secondly, a border around the layout will be raised slightly above the height of the actual train table where it is flat. This helps to keep scenic elements such as ground foam and ballast from accidentally being brushed off the train table when they are applied to the layout. Lastly, the border will cover the 1x4 wood sides of the base of the train table as well as the cross-sections of the plywood and Homasote layers on the top of the train table.

For the material to create the border, you will need a thin, sturdy board such as Masonite or Lauan in 1/4 inch thickness. The good news is that since you purchased a four-by-eight-foot sheet for the construction of the divider in the last chapter, you should have some left over, which can now be used for the train table border. Since the Lauan has a wood grain finish,

The application of the extra pieces of backdrop will serve as a transition to where the mountain will be located.

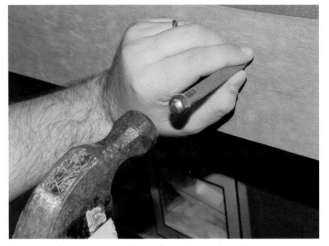

Using a nail set when attaching nails to the border will keep the hammer from damaging the wood.

you can, as I did, apply wood stain on it when finished, which gives the border a professional look. Some model railroaders, however, prefer to paint this border a dark color when finished, so feel free to do whatever you like best.

It is neither necessary nor advisable to cut the border pieces to the entire length of the layout table, since the height of the border will vary around the layout. Instead, cut pieces to fit appropriate sections such as mountains or level. As you can see from the illustration, the area where the mountain containing the tunnel is located has a very high border. It is important that you know in advance how high your mountains will be so that you can make the proper measurements for cutting the border.

To avoid splintering when cutting the wood, use a fine cut blade for your saw. If you have access to a table saw, so much the better: it will produce the best results on the long, straight-edge cuts – but a circular saw will do a fine job, too. For the areas where the terrain will vary in height, cut rectangular pieces so that the height of the entire piece equals the maximum height that the terrain will be. Once the pieces are cut into rectangles, lightly mark with a pencil the contour change of the terrain. Then, using a jigsaw with a fine blade, slowly cut along this line to avoid excess splintering of the wood. You may want to use a file or some sandpaper to smooth off the rough edges after you make the cuts.

Once all the cuts are complete, fasten the borders to the train table using 1" finish nails. To avoid damaging the wood when pounding the nails into place, use a nail set (this tool allows you to pound the nail flush with the board without leaving those unsightly dents from the head of the hammer). Connect the borders directly to the one-by-four base around the edge of the base of the table top. Another option is to

use small, 1" wood screws to fasten the border instead. Keep in mind, though, that the screws will be more visible than finish nails, but they may be necessary to adequately support the taller sections of the border.

Using the same steps from the last chapter to fasten them securely, I applied the excess backdrop pieces on the border on the side of the layout where the large mountain will go. The background transitions on both sides of the mountain create the useful visual illusion that the mountain is larger than it actually is.

With all the borders attached, the layout may take on a strange look, especially in the areas where the borders stick up above the layout. Keep in mind that they will serve the purpose of providing a support for the mountains that we will build in the next section.

Mountains

If you choose to include mountains on your model railroad, you'll want to try to capture the splendor and majestic beauty that actual ones possess – only on a smaller scale. It isn't difficult to construct a mountain that doesn't resemble a real mountain so much as it resembles a mound of formless plaster – but the good news is that with Woodland Scenics' excellent materials, tools, and clear instructions, it's *easy* to make great looking, realistic mountains for your model railroad … the kind you'll be proud to show visitors and friends.

A good idea before you get started is to observe real mountains. If you don't live near a real mountain range, try books or magazines in order to get a feel for the real thing. If you are modeling a particular railroad (such as the Santa Fe) or region (such as Raton Pass), it might be wise to view a train video with footage of the actual railroad and/or region, paying close attention to the background – especially the color of the rocks and dirt, along with the types of trees in that particular area. The key is to get a clear image of what real mountainous terrain looks like, and use this vision during the construction.

Sub-terrain:

Building the Tunnel

In the previous chapter, you made pencil marks on the train table where the mountains and tunnel portals will be located. The first part of building your mountain involves the creation of the sub-terrain and the tunnel. We'll start with the tunnel portals.

Following your pencil marks on the train table, use Woodland Scenics Foam Tack Glue to attach the two pieces of foam to the train table. Then, use some more Foam Tack Glue to attach the tunnel portal to the foam, being careful to place it in the correct position you determined when you previously tested for prop-

Use 1" pieces of foam to construct the tunnel. Be sure to run several trains through to check for clearance before permanently attaching pieces in place with Foam Tack Glue.

Once the pieces of foam have been cut and fit into place, use Foam Tack Glue to permanently attach them together.

Slightly indent each level as you work your way up the moutain. Don't worry about holes and gaps as these will be covered later on with Woodland Scenics Plaster Cloth.

Use the Woodland Scenics Hot Wire Foam Cutter to shave the foam to the shape you desire.

er clearances. Since Foam Tack Glue is a contact type adhesive, it should hold the tunnel portal in place very quickly, but you may still want to temporarily apply a little masking tape to help the tunnel portals stay upright while the Foam Tack Glue dries.

To create the actual tunnel, you'll be making a long-box-type covering over the track, upon which the rest of the mountain will be built. Construct the interior part of the tunnel with a sheet of 1"-thick foam, using the top and sides of the tunnel portal as starting points. When cutting these pieces of foam, remember to leave plenty of room inside the tunnel for clearance purposes.

After you cut the pieces of foam, temporarily lay them in place and use Woodland Scenics Foam Nails to hold them together. At this point, it is a good idea to run some of your M.T.H. Electric Trains through the tunnel to make sure they don't brush or hit the inside of the tunnel walls. When you are satisfied, take the tunnel apart and paint the surface of the foam that faces the inside of the tunnel black. (Just about any black latex paint will do the trick here; what's important is that we take care of this step now ... it is much more difficult to paint the inside of the tunnel after the mountain has been constructed.) Once the paint is dry, fasten the pieces of foam together again using Woodland Scenics Foam Nails or Foam Tack Glue.

Foam Mountain Foundation

With the tunnel complete, you can turn your attention to constructing the sub-terrain (or underneath foundation) of the mountain. This can be done two different ways: using wadded up newspaper with masking tape holding it in place, or foam layered and cut to shape. For the two large mountains on the

Santa Fe Raton Pass Railroad, I chose to use the foam method.

Using the Woodland Scenics Foam Knife, cut large blocks from the 4" sheet of foam and place them, following the pencil outlines on the train table, around the perimeter of the mountain. It is a good idea to cut the foam pieces a little larger than the outlines, so you have more to work with when cutting the foam and shaping the mountain later on. At this point, don't worry if there are gaps between other pieces of foam or other items such as the tunnel portal or backdrop, as they will be filled in later.

When you are satisfied with the first layer, use some Foam Tack Glue to permanently attach it to the train table. You should have a minute or so to slide the pieces of foam around into the correct position before the glue sets them in place. Repeat this process using blocks of foam to build the mountain upward, slightly indenting each layer much like a pyramid. In order to accomplish this, you will find it necessary to place a few blocks on the top of the tunnel you just created. You need not worry about this, as the foam is lightweight yet very strong and will easily be able to handle the load.

The main mountain on the Santa Fe Raton Pass Railroad is high and skinny, due to the divider with the background transitioning into the mountain. I consider this to be one of the advantages of using the divider, as it allows us to create a mountain without taking up much real estate on the layout. As you can see, this is very important when space is limited.

For the final shaping of the mountain structure, use a Woodland Scenics Hot Wire Foam Cutter. This is a great tool – whether you are constructing one large mountain or multiple mountains on your layout. The Hot Wire Foam Cutter is easy to use – just plug it in, hold the trigger on the handle, and pull the wire through the foam. That's all there is to it! Again, don't worry at this point about the gaps – instead, focus on the overall shape of the mountain.

Note: You may be tempted to use the blue home construction foam available at your local home improvement store. **Don't!** *When you use a hot wire cutter on this type of material, it emits toxic fumes that can be harmful if you don't have proper ventilation. When using Woodland Scenics Foam you don't have to worry about this, as it does not emit dangerous fumes.*

Plaster Cloth Hard Shell

The next step, involving the use of Woodland Scenics Plaster Cloth, is much like putting the siding on a house. Plaster Cloth is a plaster-coated cloth designed especially for terrain modeling. It comes in 8x15 rolls, and all you have to do is simply cut with scissors, dip in water, and lay it in place. Although it is very easy to use, water may drip on the layout as you're working; to prevent too much of a mess or

Woodland Scenics Plaster Cloth comes in convenient rolls. All you need to do is cut, dip in water, and drape in place. Overlap each piece by 50 percent and use a brush to smooth out the plaster on the cloth.

even damage, put large strips of masking tape on all track near the mountain *before you begin*. It's also a good idea to temporarily place some type of covering over the divider background – Saran® Wrap, held gently in place with masking tape, works well.

To work with the Plaster Cloth, you will need some scissors and a large rectangular pan or dish.

Since lightweight Hydrocal hardens rather quickly, apply a few rocks at a time. Number the rocks with their corresponding locations on the mountains.

After applying the rocks to the mountain, you may need some filler for certain areas. The dark areas on the mountain are from another Woodland Scenics product called Mold-A-Scene.

Plaster Cloth comes in convenient rolls that allow you to cut off pieces in the size you need as you go along. After cutting a piece, simply dip it in water for 1-2 seconds and lay in place with the bumpy side up. It will adhere to the contours of the foam underneath. Repeat this process, being sure to overlap each piece by 50 percent. Use a small paintbrush to smooth and spread out the plaster on the Plaster Cloth, especially where two pieces overlap. When you come to a layout border edge, simply fold the end of the Plaster Cloth over and tuck it up against the edge using your brush once again to spread the plaster against the border. Continue this process until every area of the mountain is covered with at least two pieces of Plaster Cloth. Allow the Plaster Cloth to dry for 30 minutes, or longer. When it dries, it will be very strong and durable, providing an excellent base for the application of other scenic elements such as rocks, color tinting, and trees.

Creating Rocks and Outcroppings

At this point, the mountain probably looks a little too smooth compared to the real thing ... it needs a few rough edges. Putting rocks and outcroppings on your mountain will do the trick. Woodland Scenics provides the model railroader with 15 different rock molds in all shapes and sizes. To make your rocks and outcroppings, fill the mold with Woodland Scenics Lightweight Hydrocal, a plaster-type material that, when mixed with water, hardens within 10 to 15 minutes.

Before you begin, mix up a batch of what is referred to as "wet water." Wet water is simply a mixture of two drops of liquid soap – such as hand or dishwashing soap – in about six ounces of water. The wet water serves to help the Lightweight Hydrocal release from the mold once it is dry. Put the wet water into a Woodland Scenics Scenic Spray bottle, and lightly spray the inside of all the rock molds you plan to use.

Colors	Mixing Ratio
Black, Raw Umber and Slate Gray	1 teaspoon pigment to 5 1/2 ounces water or 1 part pigment to 32 parts water.
Burnt Umber, Concrete, Stone Gray, Yellow Ocher and White	2 teaspoons pigment to 5 1/2 ounces water or 1 part pigment to 16 parts water.

Now you're ready to make the mold material, itself. Simply follow the directions on the side of the Lightweight Hydrocal box: add water, according to the amount that you want to make, and then mix together using a spatula. When mixed to a soup-like consistency, pour it into the rock molds; don't allow bubbles to form. Let the rock molds sit for roughly 30 minutes. Once dry, carefully press against the rubber side of the molds to pop out the newly formed rocks.

One of the great attributes of the Lightweight Hydrocal is that it is lightweight, yet very strong. But it's also incredibly easy to shape with a knife or other carving instrument (such as a spoon!), and is very easy to color.

After you have made several rocks and outcroppings from the molds and allowed them to dry properly, you are ready to place them on the mountain. You will start this by "fitting" them where you want them to go. If they don't seem to fit well, simply take a spoon and carve the back or the side to fit the area where you want it to go. You may even want to purposely break a larger rock into two pieces in order to fit them in place. Don't worry about making them perfectly flush yet; you'll take care of that when actually attaching the rocks to the mountain. When you have settled on a location for a particular rock, write a number on the backside of the rock, and on the mountain where the rock will go, write that same number. Pairing numbered rocks with numbered locations will make it much easier when it comes time to attach them all to the mountain. Continue this process until you have fitted and numbered enough rocks for the mountain to look realistic. Remember, though, that different mountains will have differing amounts and sizes of rocks and outcroppings, so you don't need to cover the entire mountain. You'll soon be adding other elements, such as trees, grass, and bushes, to the terrain.

Now you're ready to mix up the glue you'll use to attach the rocks and outcroppings to the mountain. Mix some more Lightweight Hydrocal in a bowl, but this time, make it thicker by adding a little less water. Keep in mind that the Lightweight Hydrocal will start hardening in only a few minutes, so mix small

amounts – only enough for about five or six rocks at a time. Next, dip the rocks in a large bowl of water for one or two seconds to get them thoroughly wet, and moisten the mountain with your Woodland Scenics Sprayer: getting the rocks and the mountain wet helps the bonding process. Now, pour the Lightweight Hydrocal directly from your mixing bowl onto the back of the rock, and press the rock into place on the mountain. To get the realistic look you want, apply a little more of the Lightweight Hydrocal with a spoon or your fingers, and fill it in around edges or between rocks. If you apply too much, just use the Woodland Scenics Scenic Sprayer at a close range to wash away the excess Lightweight Hydrocal. When working around areas such as the tunnel portal, you can use the Lightweight Hydrocal to fill in any gaps or spaces there, as well. When you're done gluing, allow everything ample time to dry – overnight, if possible – before proceeding to the next step.

Coloring the Mountain

With all the physical features such as rocks and outcroppings on your mountain in place, the next step involves transforming it from the plain white of the Lightweight Hydrocal into the realistic mountain shades of brown, black, and gray. The Woodland Scenics Earth Color Kit is a great tool to accomplish this task. It provides one small bottle of each of the eight different color pigments along with a mixing tray, foam applicator, and complete instructions. Depending on the size of your mountain, you may want to use larger bowls for mixing the color pigments. And, if you are building a larger layout with many mountains, you may want to get additional larger bottles of the color pigments you plan to use.

To start coloring the mountain, mix the Burnt Umber at a 16 to 1 ratio (16 parts of water and 1 part Burnt Umber). Using the foam applicator or a small paintbrush, dab spots of color on the rocks and Lightweight Hydrocal shell; this technique is called "leopard spotting." Your goal here is to cover about half of the mountain with the color, so it resembles leopard's fur. As you work with the Burnt Umber, you

Using the technique called leopard spotting, color only half of the mountain with Burnt Umber (or whichever color you choose).

Fill in the open areas with Yellow Ocher. If more color is needed, just put on another application. Don't forget to lock the color in place with Scenic Cement.

may notice that the coloring seems very light. If this is the case, simply apply more color on that particular area to make it darker. I have found that it is much easier to *add* more color than to take it off. But don't worry: If you do happen to get it too dark, one of the great attributes of color pigments is that you can just spray on some water to wash it off and then start the

process over again until you get the desired result. It is virtually mistake-proof.

When you're done with the Burnt Umber, mix Yellow Ocher at the same 16 to 1 ratio you used for the Burnt Umber. Using the foam applicator or a paintbrush, apply the Yellow Ocher in the white areas on the mountain you haven't colored yet ... until the whole mountain is covered with one of the two colors. (A bit of overlapping of colors adds to an overall appearance of realism.)

The next color to be added is black. Since black is such a strong color, mix it with water at a 32 to 1 ratio. Starting lightly and getting darker as you go along, apply the black to the entire mountain using the foam applicator. The black will seep into the crevices and cracks, bringing out the details of the rocks very vividly, and giving the mountain terrain greater depth.

Feel free to use other colors in the Earth Color Kit, especially if you are trying to match a particular shade from the region you are modeling. The *Woodland Scenics Scenery Manual* has several great illustrations showing different combinations of the color pigments and what the result looks like.

Since color pigments don't contain any acrylic binders, they will fade with time and exposure to light and air. To prevent fading, seal the colors in place with Woodland Scenics Scenic Cement. Scenic Cement is easily applied using a spray bottle – just be sure to spray the area completely. Keep in mind, though, that once you use the Scenic Cement, you will not be able to wash off the colors and start over – they are "locked" in place. However, if you do decide you want to add more colors on top of the Scenic Cement layer, you can do that! Just apply the additional color and add another layer of Scenic Cement spray when you are done to lock that additional coloring in place.

Scenery:

Ground Cover

At this point the mountain is really starting to look much more realistic, although its transformation is not quite complete. The mountain needs some scenery.

It is important, at this point, to differentiate between the terms "ground cover" and "scenery." Ground cover refers to natural vegetation and the soil that it grows in, while scenery includes ground cover as well as other elements such as rocks, water, and roads.

The very first step you should take is to look around outside or in books with pictures of the region you are modeling; doing so will help you to get an idea of what you want the scenery to look like on your model railroad. You'll probably notice that in nature, rarely do you find uniform vegetation and color with the exception of maybe a lawn in front of a house. Since our goal is realistic scenery, scatter various colors

Woodland Scenics carries many different types of turf in either bags or these handy shaker bottles that make application very easy.

After spraying the top of the mountain with Scenic Cement, I simply sprinkled Burnt Grass Turf on. I then locked it in place by respraying with Scenic Cement.

Apply a dab of Hob-e-Tac directly to the location you want to place a bush or other type of foliage. Wait 15 minutes and then press it in place.

and heights of vegetation on your model railroad.

Undercoat

Earth Blend and Green Blend are especially important undercoat colors for the non-mountainous areas, such as fields, hills, and areas around bodies of water, on your layout. And, if you discover an area of your layout that wasn't painted, remedy it now by applying these undercoat colors. Mix them with water and use the foam applicator or paintbrush to apply them. When you are satisfied with the color, be sure to use the Scenic Cement to lock the colors in place.

Turf and Soil

Different types of real mountains have differing amounts of turf showing. In fact, turf coverage can even vary on the same mountain from one side to the other. Adding some turf vegetation and soil is the next step in making your model mountain even more realistic. Toward that end, Woodland Scenics provides two types of ground foam turf that you can use: fine and coarse. Start out with the fine and then work in some of the coarse. It couldn't be much easier: Spray selected areas with some Scenic Cement and then sprinkle the turf on. If you happen to get too much on, simply brush the excess off. Once you are satisfied, lock the turf in place by re-spraying it with the Scenic Cement.

It's a good idea, when applying ground foam turf, to use more than one color. For example, cover an area with Medium Green turf. Then lightly sprinkle another color of turf such as Burnt Grass. This will bring contrast to the area and give it depth, which adds a realistic effect. Once again, if you get too much on or don't like the way it looks, then just brush it off, and start over.

Bushes and Other Foliage

In addition to turf, many mountains have other vegetation on them such as bushes and tall grass. To re-create these on your mountain, you can utilize Woodland Scenics products such as Foliage Clusters, Bushes, and Clump Foliage, all of which are made with ground foam. You can also use another Woodland Scenics product call Lichen – an organic material that comes in a variety of colors.

Whichever product you choose, application is very simple. Using the brush applicator in the lid, apply some Hob-e-Tac adhesive to the area and then press the product in place. If applying on a steep slope, wait about 10 to 15 minutes after applying the Hob-e-Tac to allow it to become very sticky before applying the bush or other foliage. This will help to ensure that the item stays in place.

Of course, real-life bushes and foliage are not uniform in color, so consider spraying some Scenic Cement on and sprinkling some Fine Turf in a different color to add definition and depth to bushes. Burnt Grass works really well for this. Re-spray with more Scenic Cement to lock it into place.

It is easy to go overboard, adding bushes and other foliage everywhere. If you refer back to those pictures of real mountains, you'll notice that many bushes are located where there are cracks, ledges, and crevices in the rock. It's helpful, too, to occasionally step back from the area you are working on. When working on a specific area you tend to be up very close; stepping back allows you to get a picture that is more representative of what a person who is observing the layout will see.

Talus (Rock Debris)

Now is a good time in the process of constructing your mountain to add Woodland Scenics Talus. In nature, talus is simply rock of various sizes broken off other larger rocks through the natural processes of freezing, thawing, and erosion. It is also referred to as rock debris. Talus is found below large rock outcroppings, around tunnel portals, at the base of rock cuts, low-lying areas, and around streams.

Since talus is broken off from other rocks, it is important to try to match the color to those on your layout. Though Woodland Scenics offers a variety of talus colors, you may want to apply your own coloring. To paint your own talus, spread it out on a flat surface (such as cardboard) and apply the color pigments the same way that you did in the section on Rocks and Outcroppings (page 67).

When the talus is dry, just sprinkle it in place in the location that you want. If it looks good, lock it into place by spraying it with Scenic Cement. One good trick is to add a little Woodland Scenics Soil Fine Turf on before spraying the Talus with Scenic Cement. This way, when you do spray the Scenic Cement on, it will wash the Soil Fine Turf into the crevices, giving the talus depth and a more realistic, dirty appearance.

Trees

Trees are the last scenic element you'll add to your mountain. Woodland Scenics provides the model railroader with a choice of Ready Made Realistic Trees or Realistic Tree Kits for those who want to make trees themselves. Of course, the Realistic Tree Kits are less expensive, so if you are planning to add many trees to your layout, you will probably want to go this route.

Ramdomly apply Talis and other debris, such as Woodland Scenics Dead Fall, on or around a mountain to help simulate real life.

To begin with a tree kit, take one of the flat tree armatures and twist it into a three-dimensional shape. Next, apply plenty of Hob-e-Tac adhesive to all the branches of the tree armature using the application brush attached to the inside of the cap. You don't need to use a ton of Hob-e-Tac, but rather just get a light coating on the branches. Since you will need to wait about 15 minutes for the Hob-e-Tac to get tacky, you can use this time to set the armature upright. Use several pieces of excess foam (left over from when you made the mountain), and poke the base of the tree armature into the foam to allow it to stand upright. A good trick here is to apply Hob-e-Tac to about a dozen tree armatures at a time. Since it takes about a minute per tree to brush the Hob-e-Tac on, by the time you are done with the last one, the first tree will be tacky enough to proceed to the next step.

Lastly, you simply hold the base of the tree armature and dip it into your bag of Clump Foliage (the Clump Foliage included in the kit may be in large pieces so you may want to tear it into smaller pieces depending on the size of the trees you are making). Pull the tree armature out and *presto!* You have a good-looking tree. If there are any excess pieces of Clump Foliage hanging on, just tear them off and throw them back in the bag for use on the next tree. Since the Clump Foliage is uniform in color, sprinkle some Fine Turf, such as Burnt Grass, on it. To finish, spray the tree with Scenic Cement to lock everything in place.

When placing trees on your layout, there are two important points to remember. The first is that you should mix trees of different heights together. Rarely in nature do you see trees of the same height, so the same should be true on your layout. Of course, in a particular area, the majority of the trees can be of the same height, but do mix in a smaller or larger one every so often to make it look realistic.

Secondly, when placing trees on a mountain, it is important to work from larger to smaller. Starting at

Placing large trees at the base and gradually smaller ones as you work your way up the mountain is an excellent example of using forced perspective. It creates the illusion of depth and distance, thus making your layout seem larger.

the base, use your largest trees. As you place trees up the mountain, use smaller and smaller trees, reserving the smallest ones for the very top. Graduating tree sizes in this way helps to produce the illusion of greater distance, and makes the mountain seem larger than it really is.

To attach the tree to the mountain, you have two choices: use the tree armature base or glue it directly to the terrain. On the Santa Fe Raton Pass Railroad, I chose to do a mix of both. Using the tree armature

Woodland Scenics Realistic Tree Kits are easy as – 1) twist the tree armature; 2) apply Hob-e-Tac adhesive and 3): dip the armature in the bag of foliage and pull it out. Presto! A great looking, easy to make tree

bases, I applied Hob-e-Tac to the bottom, waited 15 minutes, and stuck it in place. Since the base has a small hole, it is then very easy to stick the tree in place. For the other trees, I simply poked a small hole in the Lightweight Hydrocal shell with a small screwdriver or awl. I then brushed some Hob-e-Tac adhesive in the hole and again waited 15 minutes before putting the tree in place. You may need to hold the tree upright for a few moments for the Hob-e-Tac to set properly.

At this point, you should have a very strikingly realistic mountain completed on your layout. A well-done mountain adds greatly to the believability of your layout.

Other Scenic Elements:

Terrain Cuts

Along with mountains and hills, terrain cuts make great additions to your model layout. Most real railroads have to travel over very uneven areas of terrain. In order to minimize the up and down elevation changes and the resulting extra fuel consumption by engines, railroads often made large cuts through sides of hills to even out the high areas, and then used the earth dug from these cuts to fill in the low area the track needed to travel across.

You can employ this terrain feature on your model layout very easily using many of the same Woodland Scenics products along with the techniques mentioned in the section on creating the mountain. On the Santa Fe Raton Pass Railroad I created two such terrain cuts at opposite corners of the layout.

To begin, cut the layout border edge to the height desired of your terrain cut. I chose a height of roughly 3" for the highest point. Since this point was at the very corner, I drew a gently sloping, jagged line from the top point down to the level of the table top. Using a jigsaw with a fine blade (remember your safety glasses), carefully cut the border board, and attach it to the side of the train table.

Next, fill the cut. For this you can use either the foam method, which you employed earlier on the mountain, or wadded-up newspaper. On the Santa Fe Raton Pass Railroad, I chose to use the wadded-up newspaper for the terrain cuts. I placed several wads up against the border, and put a couple of long pieces of masking tape over them to hold them in place. I followed by using the Plaster Cloth to cover the entire area of the terrain cut, making sure that each strip was tucked under at the border as well as overlapping the cloth to produce a strong shell once it dried.

Next, add rocks and outcroppings, and then color them all using the various color pigments from Woodland Scenics Earth Color Kit. Follow up the coloring by adding Woodland Scenics Fine Turf along with some Clump Foliage. And don't forget the Scenic

Using wadded up newspaper held in place by masking tape, drape Woodland Scenics Plaster Cloth over the area. Next, spread the plaster on the cloth with a paint brush. When dry, it provides a strong foundation for other scenery.

Well done terrain cuts like this one can greatly add to the scenic impact of your layout.

The Homasote top is sturdy, yet soft enough to carve with a utility knife.

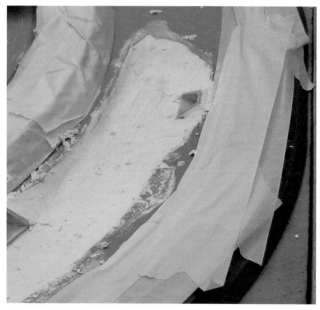

Mix a small batch of Lightweight Hydrocal to fill in the base of the stream. Gently slope it up to the edges of the cut Homasote.

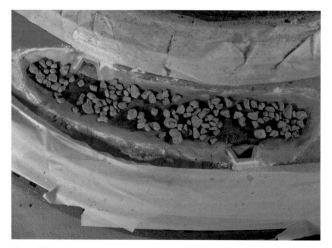

Start filling the stream with Extra Coarse Talis as shown. Note: the base of the stream was colored prior to this step.

Cement to lock everything in place. Finally, add a few trees and you've just turned a boring corner of your model railroad layout into an exciting area full of realistic scenery for your M.T.H. Electric Trains to pass by.

Creating a Small Stream

Most people think of streams, rivers, or ponds when adding water to their model railroads. A quick look around, though, reveals that water exists in a variety of places in real life – gullies, drainage ditches, puddles next to a building – giving you a lot of creative potential for your layout. To preserve realism, keep in mind that a railroad in the Northwest United States is likely to have much more rainfall and more water around than a railroad that travels through the Arizona desert.

Woodland Scenics has three different water products to meet your water modeling needs, including Realistic Water, E-Z Water, and Water Effects (for items such as waterfalls). All of them produce excellent results and are very easy to use – especially Realistic Water, which is what I chose to use on the Santa Fe Raton Pass Railroad for the small stream between the two tracks located on the Wootton Curve.

To begin, I drew the location of the stream directly on the train table and then removed the track from the table. Since water usually rests in low-lying areas, I needed to create such an area. The nice part of using Homasote on the top of the train table is that you can easily cut and carve it. Using a utility knife, I carefully cut along my drawn lines at a 45-degree angle. I followed this by using a flat-edged screwdriver to gently pry pieces of the Homasote up. Don't worry if you cut beyond the drawn lines or if it doesn't look neat – the important task is to remove the Homasote all the way down to the plywood.

Once the Homasote is removed, the next step in this process involves constructing culverts to hold the water. Woodland Scenics provides a variety of culverts to choose from, including concrete, rock, stone, and wood. All of the culverts are made from high-density plaster castings, and are base-color white. Apply the concrete color included in the Coloring Kit in the same manner as the other colors on your terrain before assembling them together with white glue.

Woodland Scenics produces their culverts in several scales, which is a great thing for those of us with O gauge M.T.H. Electric Trains. The different scales allow us choose according to our needs. I did this on the Santa Fe Raton Pass Railroad as I utilized the Concrete N Scale Culverts. Since the Homasote is only about a 1/2" thick, using a larger sized one would make the culvert's height surpass the top of the track – which would have looked very strange. The N scale culverts were small enough to fit down in the cut-out

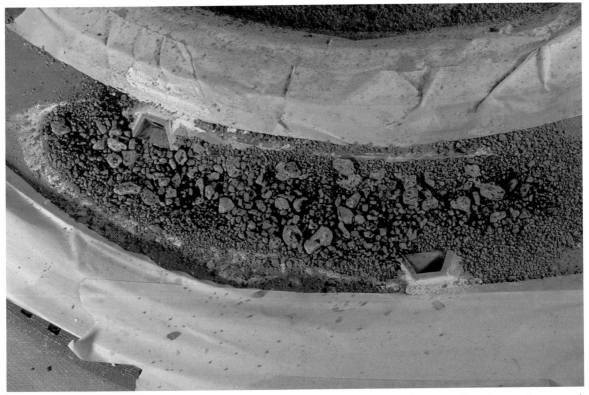

Continue the process by adding different sized Talis and Soil Fine Turf. If the rocks are level, use your finger to move them around to create the low area in the middle of the stream.

Hold the bottle close to the stream when pouring Woodland Scenics Realistic Water to avoid air bubbles. Apply a 1/8" layer. If you want deeper "water," add a second application after the first is dry.

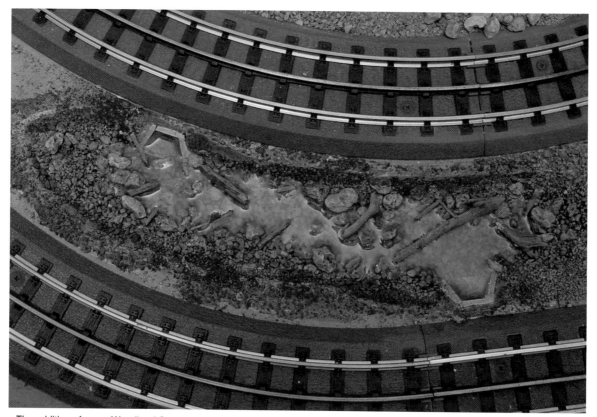

The addition of some Woodland Scenics Dead Fall while the Realistic Water is still wet adds to the realism of the stream.

area in order to maintain a realistic look.

With the culverts colored and glued together, place them in their correct position down in the cutout area of the Homasote. Follow this by mixing a small batch of Lightweight Hydrocal, using a little less water to give it the consistency of thick soup. Spoon the Lightweight Hydrocal into the areas along the backside of the culverts. If you get any on the culvert, use a damp rag to wipe it off before it hardens. Spread the remaining Lightweight Hydrocal out on a thin layer over the plywood and along the cut edges of the Homasote, creating a nice slope down toward the middle part of the stream. Be sure to leave enough space in the stream area for the addition of rocks later on. Let the Lightweight Hydrocal set for at least 30 minutes before continuing to the next step.

Once the Lightweight Hydrocal is dry, color the deepest part of the streambed the darkest, applying lighter shades toward the edges of where the water will be. Don't forget to spray it with Scenic Cement to lock in the color when you have it just how you want it.

Since most streams contain rocks, sand, and fine soil, add these to the stream, as well. The trick is to start large and work your way down to the smaller sizes. I suggest beginning this task by adding talus fol-

lowed by either Soil or Earth Fine Turf. When you are satisfied with the look, spray on the Scenic Cement to lock it in place. You may want to follow this up by using the foam applicator and dabbing a little of the black color pigment on the rocks to help bring out the details of the rocks. Spray on some Scenic Cement when you are finished adding the color to the rocks.

The last step in creating your stream also happens to be the easiest – adding the water. With everything in place, simply pour a 1/8" layer of the Woodland Scenics Realistic Water into the stream, being sure to hold the bottle close to the table to avoid forming air bubbles. Allow at least 24 hours for the Realistic Water to dry. If you want deeper water, add anoterh 1/8" laye rof the Realistic Water.

Constructing Railroad Crossings

Even though model railroad enthusiasts may not focus as much upon roads as they do upon railroad tracks, the addition of realistic roads will add yet another important dimension of realism to your layout – and most roads on model railroads inevitably end up crossing over railroad tracks at some point. These railroad crossings can vary from wood timber to vulcanized rubber to concrete. For the Santa Fe Raton Pass

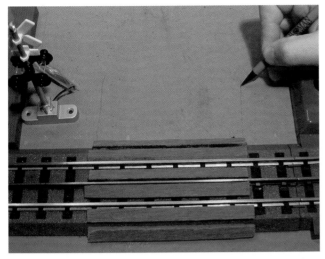

Temporarily place the pieces of wood you plan to use for the crossing before you mark the location of your roads with a pencil.

It is important to test run one of your M.T.H. engines over each crossing to make sure it doesn't lose electrical conductivity to the center rail. If it does, simply file down the pieces of wood before permanently attaching them in place.

Railroad, I chose to use wood timber for all of my railroad track crossings.

I started this process by gathering some of the excess pieces of Lauan wood board that was used to create the divider and layout border edge. Using Lauan for the railroad crossings has several advantages. First, it already has a wood grain so all it will need is a little coloring or dark stain to make it look like a real piece of wood timber. Secondly, 1/4" Lauan is just about perfect for making crossings on M.T.H. RealTrax, as it matches the height of the rails when laid flat. Lastly, Lauan also takes paint very well in the event that you want to do other types of crossings such as concrete or vulcanized rubber.

To start, you will need to cut the Lauan into 3/8"-wide strips. The length will depend on how wide your crossing is, and whether you want to utilize multiple

pieces across it. I used a 5"-length on the crossing for the Santa Fe Raton Pass Railroad.

Next, color the strips of cut Lauan. You can do this by using some brown paint or a very dark wood stain.

The last step involves putting the strips of Lauan in place. A key when placing them is to make sure that strips of Lauan next to the center rail do not rise above the top of the center rail. If this happens, then the electrical roller pickup on your M.T.H. Engine will loose power from the track and stop each time it goes over the crossing area. To correct this, use a file or a piece of sandpaper on the bottom side of the strip of Lauan to make it fit properly. On the outside of the outer rails, you can butt the strip of Lauan directly against the rails. You may need to file or sand the strip of Lauan down a bit for it to fit correctly here, as well. When you are satisfied with the placement of the strips of wood, use white glue to attach them directly to the M.T.H. RealTrax.

Roads and Crossings

Roads, much like rialroad tracks, were built with the purpose of connecting places, such as towns and industries. A quick look around, and you will see that real roads often run right next to railroad tracks, or cross over them. Roads also come in various sizes and types such as dirt, gravel, asphalt, and concrete. Keep this in mind as you plan where roads will be placed on your model railroad.

Concrete and Asphalt Roads

The Woodland Scenics Road System is a tremendous product that makes it easy to produce very realistic-looking concrete or asphalt roads on your model

Woodland Scenics Paving Tape is easy to apply – just peel off the backing and stick it in place.

Mix Woodland Scenics Smooth-It with water and pour it in place. Use a straight edge to level it between the pieces of Paving Tape. When dry, you may want to gently sand it to smooth any rough spots.

To color your roads, just pour some of the Woodland Scenics Top Coat coloring (Concrete or Asphalt) and spread it out with a brush or foam applicator.

railroad layout. The major advantage compared to pre-cut tarpaper road sections is that the Road System allows you to place roads anywhere, at any angle that you desire, over virtually any terrain. Coloring the Road System is easy, too, and you can make roads look old, new, or somewhere in-between. The System consists of just three items: Paving Tape, Smooth-It, and Asphalt/Concrete Top Coat Coloring.

To begin, use a pencil to map out where your roads will be located, then apply the Paving Tape along your drawn line. Paving Tape is an adhesive-backed foam tape that will serve as an outline for your road. Next, mix some Woodland Scenics Smooth-It with water in a bowl. Smooth-It is a plaster-type material that is similar to Lightweight Hydrocal. Once

mixed, just pour the Smooth-It into the road area between your pieces of Paving Tape. Using a long, straight-edged piece of plastic that is included with the Paving Tape, place it across the road resting on the Paving Tape, then drag it along the length of the road to spread the Smooth-It evenly along the road. Once you are satisfied with the results, allow the Smooth-It to dry for 30 minutes. When dry, remove the Paving Tape.

The last step involves coloring the road. Here Woodland Scenics give the model railroader two choices: asphalt or concrete. Whichever you choose, just pour some of the Asphalt or Concrete Top coloring directly on the road and spread it out using a brush or foam applicator. Now you have a great looking road!

You can also use the Road System to create great looking sidewalks and curbs. Just follow the same procedures you did for making roads (making them much smaller, of course), and then color them with the Concrete Top Coat color.

Dirt and Gravel Roads

You can create dirt and gravel roads just as easily as paved roads. For dirt roads, simply sprinkle on some Soil or Earth Fine Turf in the area where you want your road. Seal it in place by spraying it with Scenic Cement. If it is a road that is less traveled, add some Fine Turf in Burnt Grass, Weeds, or Grass colors to simulate vegetation growth between the tire tracks.

To create gravel roads, you can use Woodland Scenics Ballast in the same manner as above. Ballast comes in a variety of colors, but I recommend you use Gray, Medium Gray, or Buff. Simply sprinkle it in place and then lock it down by spraying it with Scenic Cement.

Buildings Unlimited Building Fronts

When space on your model railroad layout is at a premium, Building Fronts from Buildings Unlimited is a valuable tool to create a thriving town in little or no space. A wide variety of Building Fronts, placed on the background attached to the divider on the Santa Fe Raton Pass Railroad, allowed me to simulate the towns of Raton and Trinidad very easily.

Buildings Unlimited Building Fronts are made of polystyrene and come molded in red and gray, allowing you to use them as they are or paint them specific colors to meet your needs. For the Santa Fe Raton Pass Railroad, my father-in-law painted several of them and added brick mortar and window-frame coloring details.

Since many of the Building Fronts have large store windows on the bottom floor, I purchased several of the printed interiors available from Buildings Unlimited

Buildings Unlimited produces a wide variety of excellent building fronts to help simulate a town in little or no space.

and attached to the back side of the Building Fronts by using a little bit of clear tape.

Upon completion of detailing the Building Fronts, I used Liquid Nails for Projects adhesive to attach them directly to the backdrop. In just a matter of minutes, I had created a town – in very little space.

One particular trick I would like to point out involves using a Buildings Unlimited Building Front as an industry for a siding in the town of Trinidad. With the siding almost up against the divider, I detailed and placed two of the Buildings Unlimited B-41 Building Side Wall Building Fronts, which come with small loading platforms and steps, placing them between the track and divider. In virtually no space, I now have an industry for my railroad to serve.

The Moreno Valley Meatpacking industry is an excellent example of how a Buildings Unlimited Building Front can be used as a location on your railroad in little or no space.

Train Control With the M.T.H. Digital Command System (DCS)

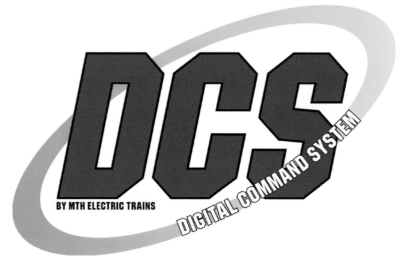

CHAPTER 8

A new era in O gauge model railroading has begun with the introduction of the M.T.H. Electric Trains Digital Command System. The Digital Command System – or DCS for short – has ushered in an exciting and extraordinary revolution that is quickly transforming the way in which we think about, and operate, our trains. DCS brings capabilities never before seen or even dreamt of and incorporates them into the hobby, providing the ultimate in realistic train operation for the model railroading enthusiast. DCS's state-of-the-art technology blended with a user-friendly interface puts you in complete control of every aspect of your model railroad, allowing you to get your trains up an running quickly and easily, regardless of whether you are building a new layout or simply connecting the system to an existing one. The result is loads of fun with over 200 features from which to choose; you'll feel as though you are inside a real train engine!

Compatibility

Probably one of the most positive aspects of DCS is that it provides compatibility within the O gauge hobby. Simply put, DCS allows products from the earliest era of the hobby to run with today's latest engines efficiently and effectively – in all operational modes – even at the same time, if you wish! This compatibility among the many types of O gauge trains is bringing the hobby together as never before through the universal train operation found only in DCS. It is the only control system to date that can perform this astounding feat, and is another prime example of M.T.H.'s leadership in innovation in the O gauge hobby.

Easy to Use

While the thought of over 200 features may scare some model railroaders, this need not be the case. Word processing programs on personal computers provide an excellent analogy: Most people can start such programs, type a simple letter, and print it very easily. However, word processors can do much more complex tasks, such as mail merges, outline numbering, and table of contents generation. Though you may never need them, they are there just in case; isn't that nice to know? The same holds true with DCS, Getting your trains up and running is rather simple and if you seek more complex train operations, they are available. It is all up to your personal tastes. However, I believe that once you start using DCS, you will begin to find new and exciting features each time, prompting you to further explore and discover features that will help push your model railroading experience to new heights of fun and realism.

The DCS User Manual and DCS "Getting Started" videotape are included with the DCS remote Control System (Item 50-1001)..

More Information on DCS

DCS is indeed a feature-rich train control system. It allows you to perform basic operations, such as sounding the whistle, along with more complex ones, such as setting pre-defined routes for your trains to travel. As a result, it would be impossible to completely cover every aspect of this amazing, jam-packed system into a single chapter. Instead, I will focus on showing you how to setup and operate DCS on the Santa Fe Raton Pass Railroad. I will walk you though this process, with clear explanations along with helpful tips, analogies, and advice that will hopefully make the DCS even easier to understand. With this information, you will be able to get your trains up and running quickly and easily when constructing your own model railroad.

Since I won't be able to cover every topic, it is very important to note that you can find complete information regarding DCS and any features not covered here in the *DCS User Manual* and *DCS Getting Started Videotape*, which are included in the DCS Remote Control System (Item 50-1001). Both are excellent sources of information, and I highly recommend that you read and watch them before getting started with DCS. An additional source of information regarding the DCS can be found on the Internet at **www.protosound2.com**. This Web site has the latest news and information, such as how to connect DCS to your

TYPES OF TRAIN CONTROL

To begin, it is very important to understand that all train control in O gauge falls into two different categories: Conventional and Command.

Control Type	Description
Conventional	This type of train control has been used since the beginning of the hobby and all trains, regardless of when they were made, can work in this mode. Conventional control is based on the raising and lowering of voltage (or electrical power) to the track. The "communication" in conventional control is between the transformer (power source) and the track. Therefore, when the voltage goes up, the train increases in speed while, on the flip side, when voltage goes down the train slows down as the engine simply responds to whatever power is available. The application of voltage to the track is much like the gas pedal on an automobile. The main drawback to this method is that all the engines respond the same way to voltage: all engines on the same track will all speed up or slow down at the same time, depending on the amount of voltage supplied to the track. To combat this, O gauge model railroaders often employ the use of electrically-insulated track sections to divide layouts into separate parts, or "blocks" as they often referred to. This allows the operator to change or vary the voltage supplied to each block, allowing for independent multiple train operation.
Command	Command control is relatively new to O gauge, and involves much greater flexibility and capability in operating model trains. This type of control applies a constant amount of voltage to the tracks – roughly 16 to 18 volts. Engines that are equipped for this type of control each have an individual "identity" and do not move when the power is initially applied to the tracks. Instead, they each wait to be given a "command" by the operator to perform a specific action. Only the engine that is being specifically referenced will respond and complete the task. The main advantage that this type of system affords is the ability to control multiple engines on the same track – commanding them to perform different tasks and travel in opposite directions at varying speeds if you choose. Furthermore, the constant voltage applied to the track allows for much smoother running at very slow speeds, and gives operators extremely realistic control of their trains.

computer in order to download the latest system updates, and sound sets for your M.T.H. ProtoSound 2.0 engines, all which allow you to easily take advantage of the latest innovations that DCS has to offer.

Which Type of Control is DCS?

As its name implies, the Digital *Command* System is a command control system, right? Yes, but it is also much more. It is true that DCS was created in conjunction with ProtoSound 2.0, providing operators with a multitude of astounding features. However, indeveloping the system, M.T.H. actually blended the two types of control, thus allowing the operator to run in either mode or even run both at the same time. It is truly a universal control system, as it has broken down the long-standing barriers of different O gauge operating systems, providing a single solution to all operating needs.

How Does DCS Work?

In the past, when the voltage was turned up on the transformer, voltage was all that ended up on the track. DCS has changed this by embedding a digital signal within the voltage going to the track. This digital signal contains the "language" that ProtoSound 2.0 engines "understand," respond and reply back to, allowing for truly interactive, two-way communication between the operator and the engine. The part that makes DCS so universal is that this digital signal does not affect conventional control engines because they cannot "hear" it, which, in turn allows DCS to control them through raising and lowering voltage.

Sound and Control Systems

To help you setup DCS and start running your trains, you must first take stock of what you have and know the capabilities of your locomotive engines. The table below examines several of main sound and control systems available on the O gauge market today.

SOUND SYSTEMS

Sound System	Type of Control	Manufacturer	Notes
Whistle/Horn	Conventional	M.T.H.	Early on, this configuration was the only one available for engines sold by M.T.H. With the introduction of ProtoSound in 1994, M.T.H. continued to offer the Whistle/Horn option for consumers into the late 1990s.
ProtoSound	Conventional*	M.T.H./QSI	The first sound system incorporated into M.T.H. engines from the factory was a huge hit. Though ProtoSound is conventional by nature, third party products are available to convert ProtoSound engines to command control via the Lionel Trainmaster Command Control System, thus allowing you to run them in Command mode with DCS.
Loco-Sounds	Conventional	M.T.H.	With the popularity of sound systems in their trains, M.T.H. developed Loco-Sounds as an option for the beginning railroader. It includes locomotive engine, whistle, and bell sounds, as well as speed control and puffing smoke in steam engines.
ProtoSound 2.0	Command	M.T.H.	As the most technologically advanced sound system in the O gauge hobby, ProtoSound 2.0 offers the operator a multitude of sound and control features, such as Passenger Station/ Freight Yard Effects, Cab Chatter, and puffing smoke synchronized to steam engine chuffing sounds.
RailSounds	Command*	Lionel	Early versions of this sound system were not equipped with Lionel's Trainmaster Command Control System (TMCC) and thus are only conventional control in nature.

The first step in setting up DCS on your layout is to become familiar with the different components. I have listed each, along with a brief description below.

Component	Description
DCS Remote Control	Use this device when controlling your trains. Its ergonomic design will help make it easy to communicate with the TIU via 900MHz signal similar to that of cordless phone and base. The DCS Remote contains an easy-to-read LCD panel and requires four AAA batteries to operate. It is included in the DCS Remote Control System (Item 50-1001) or is sold separately in the event that you want an extra unit to share with friends and family.
Track Interface Unit (TIU) Size: 10 1/4" x 7 1/2"	Known as the "brains" of DCS, this device sits between the track and the transformer and communicates with the DCS Remote. The TIU then relays those signals on to the engine via a digital signal through the tracks to the engine. It comes included in the DCS Remote Control System, (Item 50-1001) as well as being sold separately.
Accessory Interface Unit (AIU)	This device plugs into the TIU, and is used to Size: 10 1/4" x 6 1/8" control any switch or accessory wired into it. Each AIU can control up to 10 switches and 10 accessories with the ability to turn them off and on, or activating them momentarily. The AIU is sold separately (Item 50-1004).

Transformer	The transformer provides electrical power for both DCS and the trains themselves. Excellent choices include the Z-750, Z-500, and the Z-4000, which is the most powerful U.L. Listed train transformer in the O gauge market (Items 40-750, 40-500, and 40-4000, respectively). All three are produced by M.T.H. Electric Trains. For a complete list of available transformers, please refer to the Transformer Compatibility Appendix in the DCS User Manual. You should be aware that older transformers often employ circuit breakers that can take several seconds before tripping, which can cause possible damage to your DCS components in the event of a derailment. To avoid this, M.T.H. recommends that you install inline "fast-acting" fuses or circuit breakers between the older transformer and the TIU. Transformers are sold separately.

Installing DCS on the Santa Fe Raton Pass Railroad

I set up DCS in a simple format on the Santa Fe Raton Pass Railroad in order to get trains up and running quickly. This type of setup is referred to as the Quick-Start configuration. In the Quick-Start, operation of trains is performed in Command mode using only ProtoSound 2.0 engines. Later on in this chapter, I will describe changing the configuration to add the capability of running Conventional mode engines – such as ProtoSounds and LocoSounds – as well as an AIU to control accessories and switches via the DCS remote. I even show how to connect a Lionel Command Base to the TIU to allow the operation of Lionel TMCC engines in command mode.

Track Wiring

If you'll recall back in Chapter 6, I pre-wired the layout by connecting 10-inch lengths of twisted pair, 16-gauge wire to the RealTrax at five locations around the layout. I then fed them through holes drilled through the top of the train table, paying careful attention to which wire was connected to the center rail, and which one was connected to the outer rail. With this task already done, I was now ready to complete wiring the layout. The technique I used on the Santa Fe Raton Pass Railroad is referred to as a star pattern, or home-run wiring. At each wire drop, I connected additional lengths of twisted pair 16-gauge wire, and ran them all the way back to the component mounting wall I created underneath the train table. There, I installed a M.T.H. Layout Wiring Terminal Block (Item-50-1014), and connected the wires from the center rail connections on the strip above the red banana plug on the Terminal Block. I then did the same for the outer rail connections on the strip above the black banana plug.

Track power wiring on the Santa Fe Raton Pass Railroad was done using 16 guage twisted-pair speaker wire purchased at Radio Shack.

Twisted-pair wire from five track locations were connected to an M.T.H. Layout Wiring Terminal Block (Item 50-1014). I made sure that the wires from the center rail were connected to the strip above the red banana plug.

Failure to separate these wires correctly will result in a short circuit, and no trains will operate.

> **TIP:**
> The red and black banana plugs found on the Layout Wiring Terminal Block, Z-4000 Transformer, and TIU all provide for dual use: you can either plug a matching banana plug into them or partly unscrew the plug, wrapping a wire around the base and re-screwing to secure the connection.

TIU Quick-Start Installation

As the "brains" of DCS, it is important to understand the different parts of the TIU. At first glance, you'll see that the TIU has quite a few connections built into it, but you only need a few of them to get your trains up and running. (More connections will be described later in the chapter.)

On the Santa Fe Raton Pass Railroad, I started working with only two connections: the **Fixed Voltage In1** and **Fixed (DCS) Out1**. I placed the Z-4000 Transformer on the storage shelf below the layout and connected the M.T.H. Wire Harness from one of the track power connections on the Z-4000 to the TIU's **Fixed Voltage In1**. The nice part of the M.T.H. Wire Harness is that is has color-coded red and black wires with banana plugs at each end, making it very easy to connect by matching the corresponding color plugs on the Z-4000 and TIU.

Paying close attention once again to match the corresponding red and black colors correctly, I then connected wires from the **Fixed (DCS) Out1** plugs on the TIU to the plugs on M.T.H. Terminal Block that we mounted earlier. An M.T.H. Wire Harness can be used for this, though I chose to use some additional twisted pair wire for the Santa Fe Raton Pass Railroad.

Track Interface Unit (TIU)

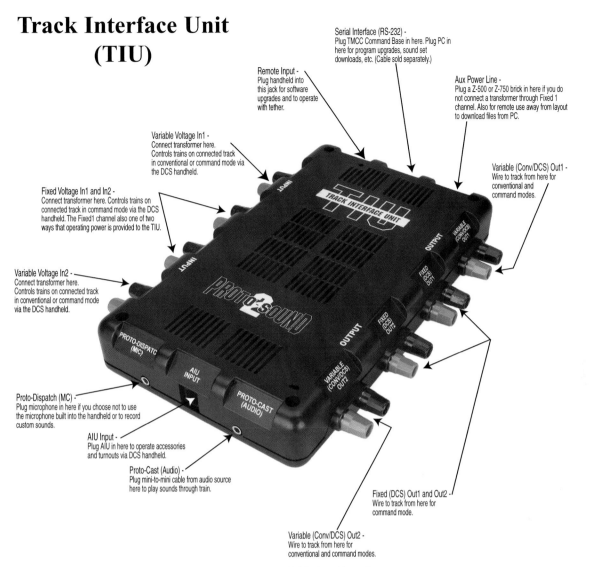

Serial Interface (RS-232) -
Plug TMCC Command Base in here. Plug PC in here for program upgrades, sound set downloads, etc. (Cable sold separately.)

Remote Input -
Plug handheld into this jack for software upgrades and to operate with tether.

Aux Power Line -
Plug a Z-500 or Z-750 brick in here if you do not connect a transformer through Fixed 1 channel. Also for remote use away from layout to download files from PC.

Variable Voltage In1 -
Connect transformer here. Controls trains on connected track in conventional or command mode via the DCS handheld.

Variable (Conv/DCS) Out1 -
Wire to track from here for conventional and command modes.

Fixed Voltage In1 and In2 -
Connect transformer here. Controls trains on connected track in command mode via the DCS handheld. The Fixed1 channel also one of two ways that operating power is provided to the TIU.

Variable Voltage In2 -
Connect transformer here. Controls trains on connected track in conventional or command mode via the DCS handheld.

Proto-Dispatch (MC) -
Plug microphone in here if you choose not to use the microphone built into the handheld or to record custom sounds.

AIU Input -
Plug AIU in here to operate accessories and turnouts via DCS handheld.

Proto-Cast (Audio) -
Plug mini-to-mini cable from audio source here to play sounds through train.

Fixed (DCS) Out1 and Out2 -
Wire to track from here for command mode.

Variable (Conv/DCS) Out2 -
Wire to track from here for conventional and command modes.

For more information regarding the various connections, refer to DCS User Manual.

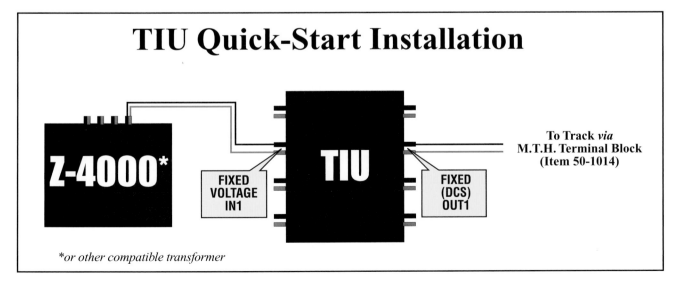

TIU Quick-Start Installation

Z-4000*

FIXED VOLTAGE IN1

TIU

FIXED (DCS) OUT1

To Track *via* M.T.H. Terminal Block (Item 50-1014)

or other compatible transformer

That's all there is to it! With this configuration, we are now ready to operate ProtoSound 2.0 engines in Command Control mode with DCS.

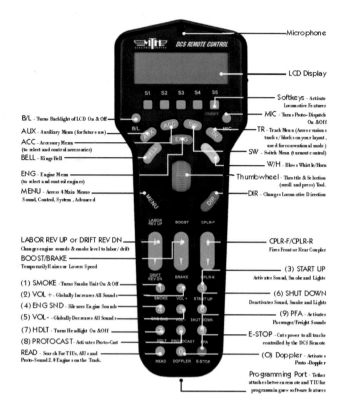

Microphone

LCD Display

Softkeys - Activate Locomotive Features

MIC - Turns Proto-Dispatch On &Off

TR - Track Menu (Access various tracks/blocks on your layout, used for conventional mode)

SW - Switch Menu (turnout control)

W/H - Blows Whistle/Horn

Thumbwheel - Throttle & Selection (scroll and press) Tool.

DIR - Changes Locomotive Direction

CPLR-F/CPLR-R Fires Front or Rear Coupler

(3) START UP Activates Sound, Smoke and Lights

(6) SHUT DOWN Deactivates Sound, Smoke and Lights

(9) PFA - Activates Passenger/Freight Sounds

E-STOP - Cuts power to all tracks controlled by the DCS Remote

(O) Doppler - Activates Proto-Doppler

Programming Port - Tether attaches between remote and TIU for programming new software features

B/L - Turns Backlight of LCD On & Off

AUX - Auxiliary Menu (for future use)

ACC - Accessory Menu (to select and control accessories)

BELL - Rings Bell

ENG - Engine Menu (to select and control engines)

MENU - Access 4 Main Menus Sound, Control, System, Advanced

LABOR REV UP or DRIFT REV DN Changes engine sounds & smoke level to labor/drift

BOOST/BRAKE Temporarily Raises or Lowers Speed

(1) SMOKE - Turns Smoke Unit On & Off

(2) VOL + - Globally Increases All Sounds

(4) ENG SND - Silences Engine Sounds

(5) VOL - - Globally Decreases All Sounds

(7) HDLT - Turns Headlight On & Off

(8) PROTOCAST - Activates Proto-Cast

READ - Search For TIUs, AIUs and Proto-Sound 2.0 Engines on the Track.

Using DCS in Command Control Mode

The DCS remote Control allows the model railroader to have complete and total control over *all* layout operations, not just engines. When used in conjunction with the AIU (sold separately), the DCS remote gives you control over switches and accessories ... eliminating the need for a control panel that often takes up valuable real estate on the train table.

When I first picked up the DCS remote, I noticed right away that it was designed to fit in my hand very comfortably, so I had single-hand control for most functions. All of the buttons, many of which are single-touch controlled, are clearly labeled for easy reference. I think the best feature, though, is the Liquid Crystal Display (LCD) panel at the top of the DCS remote. The LCD not only allows you to see the status of engines, switches and accessories, but M.T.H. has also built in a user-friendly set of menus that are easy to navigate. These menus allow the operator to simply pick and choose features, eliminating the need to remember certain button sequences to perform a task. The LCD, coupled with the consistency that M.T.H. built into the system, makes the DCS Remote easy to use – even for first time operators.

USING THE THUMBWHEEL

Action	Description
Scrolling	Gently spin the thumbwheel either up or down. This action will correspondingly move the black triangle pointer up or down on the left-side of the LCD, scrolling through the list of features from which to choose.
Pressing	Press directly down on the thumbwheel to select whichever feature is indicated by the black triangle.

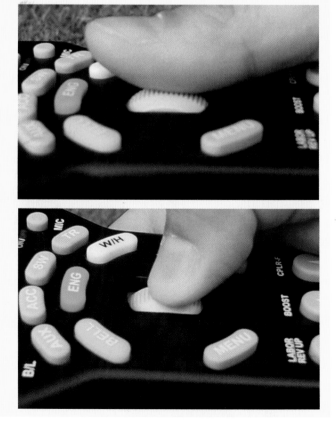

Using the Thumbwheel

In order to pick and choose among features from menus on the LCD panel of the DCS Remote, M.T.H. added a multi-function thumbwheel control. This control is found in the very center of the DCS Remote, and it offers two distinct actions.

A mouse connected to a computer serves as a good analogy for these actions. Scrolling is like moving the mouse, which in turn moves the pointer around your computer screen. Pressing is like clicking a button on your mouse so it selects whatever the pointer is on.

Powering Up DCS Components

To power up DCS Components on the Santa Fe Raton Pass Railroad, I used the following sequence:

- Turn on the Z-4000 Transformer, which also powers up the TIU (because I am using the Fixed 1 Channel; TIU channels will be discussed later in this chapter). Turn the handle of the transformer that is connected up, so the display reads between 16 and 18 volts.

- Press the On/Off button on the DCS Remote to power it up. It will take about 2-3 seconds to initialize.

TIPS:

Failure to turn the handles on the transformer to provide voltage to the TIU and track will result in "Out of Range" and "RF Error" messages on the DCS Remote.

If the DCS Remote fails to turn on, or it has trouble communicating with engines on the layout, check that the four AAA batteries are securely in place, and are sufficiently charged.

Initial ProtoSound 2.0 Engine Setup

When using ProtoSound 2.0 engines with DCS, it must go through an initial setup process. This is only done the first time you use DCS and is relatively easy to do. The steps are as follows:

- With the Z-4000 on, make sure the handles are down and the display reads 0.0 Volts

- Place a ProtoSound 2.0 engine on the track. Remove any other engines off the track.

- Turn the Z-4000 handles up so the display reads 18 Volts. The ProtoSound 2.0 engine will remain silent and dark; this is normal.

- Press the MENU button the DCS Remote.

- Use the thumbwheel to scroll to SYSTEM and press to select.

- Use the thumbwheel to scroll to ENGINE SETUP and press to select.

- Use the thumbwheel to scroll to ADD ENGINE and press to select.

- Use the thumbwheel to scroll to ADD M.T.H. ENGINE and press to select.

- The LCD will show LOOKING FOR ENGINE for a few seconds and will then automatically add it to the DCS Remote. All ProtoSound 2.0 engines have the Smart-Read feature built in that allows them to tell the TIU its name. (If you don't like the default name, you have the ability to change it. For more info, refer to the DCS User Manual.)

To add other ProtoSound 2.0 engines, repeat these steps for each one. This process adds the engines to the DCS Remote. Therefore, if you purchase an additional one for multiple user operation, you will need to repeat this process for each engine for the new DCS Remote. The good news is that this information will stay intact in the memory of the DCS Remote when you change the batteries.

Operating ProtoSound 2.0 Engines

We are now ready to start operating our M.T.H. ProtoSound 2.0 engines and experience model railroading like never before.

Getting an Engine Going

- Place one or more engines on the track. Turn up the voltage on the Z-4000 to 18 volts. You may hear a faint "click" sound come from the engine as you do. All the engines will remain silent and dark.

- Press the READ button on the DCS Remote. DCS will "look" to see what engines are on the track and place them in the Active Engine list (the top part of the engine list). All engines that were added to the DCS Remote but are not on the track are added to the Inactive Engine list.

Active vs. Inactive Engines

To help illustrate what is meant by Active and Inactive Engines, I like to use the analogy of a street and a parking lot. The street represents your layout with the cars on the street representing the engines in the Active Engine list. Some of the cars on the street are moving and some are stopped. Similarly, some of the engines on your Active Engine list are moving and some are not. The parking lot refers to Inactive Engine list. The cars in the parking lot represent the engines in the Inactive Engine list as they are turned off and stored somewhere off your train layout.

- Use the thumbwheel to scroll to the engine you want to control, and press to select it.

- The LCD will show the name of the engine you selected, along with 0 SMPH (which stands for scale miles per hour).

- Press the 3 (Start Up) button the DCS Remote to initiate the sounds and lights on the engine.

- To get the engine moving, scroll the thumbwheel upward slowly. As you do, the SMPH reading on the LCD will increase. To decrease the speed, scroll the thumbwheel downward.

> **TIPS:**
> Failure to press the 3 (Start Up) button before getting the engine moving will result in it operating what is referred to as stealth mode – it will run completely silent.
>
> If you see an accident about to occur when running your trains, hit the red E-STOP button in the very lower right-hand corner of the DCS Remote. This cuts power to the entire layout and stops all the engines instantly. Pressing the the E-STOP button will also make it necessary to power down the transformer, TIU, and DCS Remote and then power them back up to reinitialize the system before continuing to run your trains.

DCS has over 200 speed steps built into it when using ProtoSound 2.0 engines, giving the operator extremely precise control ranging from a barely noticeable creep all the way to the high speed of a hotshot passenger train.

Stopping an Engine and Changing Direction

Now that you have an engine rolling down the tracks, you will probably want to stop it and change its direction. To do this, you have two methods:

- Spin the thumbwheel down until the SMPH shows 0 on the LCD. If you spin the thumbwheel back up, the engine will continue in the same direction it was previously going.

- Press the DIR (Direction) button and spin the thumbwheel upward to start the engine going in the opposite direction.

Or:

- Press the DIR (Direction) button. If the engine is traveling semi-fast when you press the DIR button, you will hear the Squealing Brakes feature of ProtoSound 2.0 as it slows down to a halt. The faster the engine is traveling, the longer it will take to stop – just like a train in real life.

- Spin the thumbwheel upward to start the engine going in the opposite direction.

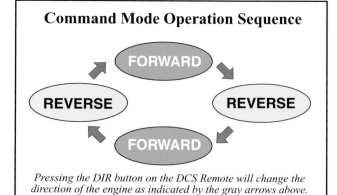

Command Mode Operation Sequence

FORWARD

REVERSE

REVERSE

FORWARD

Pressing the DIR button on the DCS Remote will change the direction of the engine as indicated by the gray arrows above.

> **TIPS:**
> Experienced hobbyists will notice the stopping distance when using the DIR button to be much longer than with previous systems. This difference is important to keep in mind when operating trains at high speeds. To give an example of this, I operated a RailKing Santa Fe E-3 at 60 SMPH around the layout. When I hit the DIR button it took roughly 6 feet of track before the engine came to a complete stop. If desired, DCS allows for this deceleration rate to be adjusted. Refer to the DCS User Manual for more information. In the event of an emergency, you can use the E-STOP button instead to stop the engines.
>
> When an engine is traveling forward and the DIR button is pressed, it comes to a stop. If you want the engine to continue going forward, simply press the DIR button again before scrolling the thumbwheel upwards to get the engine moving.

For those familiar with conventional control operation, you'll note that there is no neutral when operating in command mode. The sequence when pressing the DIR button is simply Forward-Reverse-Forward.

Controlling a Different Engine

Once you have one ProtoSound 2.0 engine moving, DCS allows you to easily select a different one, start it up, and get it moving as well. To do this, follow these steps:

- With the first engine moving, press the ENG (Engine) button

- The LCD will show the Active Engine list. Scroll the thumbwheel to the engine you want to control, and press to select it.

- The LCD will now show the name of the engine along with 0 SMPH.

- Press the 3 (Start Up) button the DCS Remote to initiate the sounds and lights on the engine.

- To get the engine moving, scroll the thumbwheel upward slowly to increase the SMPH reading on the LCD.

- To get a third and fourth engine moving, simply repeat the steps above. Let me suggest that if you run multiple engines, you may want to have them all go slow the first few times while you get accustomed to switching between engines.

"Jumping" Back to the Last Engine

Now that two engines are moving at the same time, the Jump feature can be utilized. Simply press the ENG (Engine) button. The LCD will show the Active Engine list with the black triangle selector next to the engine you were controlling prior to the current one. Press the thumbwheel down to select it. You now are controlling that engine.

Shutting Down an Engine

When an engine is stopped either by decreasing the speed to 0 SMPH or hitting the DIR button, it continues to make idle sounds. DCS provides the feature to shut down an engine. With the engine selected on the DCS Remote, just press the 6 (Shut Down) button. Quickly, you will hear the engine go through a series of shut down sounds before going silent and the lights turning off. The engine will remain on the Active Engine list on your DCS Remote since it is still on the layout.

One-Touch Functions

The DCS Remote provides several functions that can be selected with a single button press for quick activation. The list below describes the One-Touch Functions:

DCS REMOTE ONE-TOUCH FUNCTIONS

Button	Description
B/L	Turns the backlight of LCD on and off. This a great feature if your train room is dimly-lit, but be advised that this will drain the batteries in the DCS Remote faster.
MIC	Hold down to activate the Proto-Dispatch feature. When pressed, users can speak through the built-in microphone at top of DCS Remote to broadcast their voices through the ProtoSound 2.0 engine that is selected.
BELL	Turns bell on and off.
W/H	Blows the whistle/horn.
DIR	Changes engine direction.
LABOR REV UP/ DRIFT REV DN	Changes engine sounds and smoke level to labor (higher level) or drift (lower level).
BOOST/BRAKE	Pressing will temporarily raise or lower speed. The engine will return to previous speed when the button is let go.
CPLR-F/CPLR-R	Opens front or rear coupler accompanied by the sounds of a coupler opening.
(1) SMOKE	Turns smoke unit on or off. It will take a second or two before the smoke appears or dissipates.
(2) VOL+	Increases all sounds on selected engine
(3) START UP	Activates sound, smoke, and lights. This process takes a few seconds.
(4) ENG SND	Silences engine sounds. This is also known as the mute button and will silence all the engines on the layout.

(5) VOL-	Decreases all sounds on selected engine
(6) SHUT DOWN	Deactivates sound, smoke, and lights. The engine will go dark and silent.
(7) HDLT	Turns headlight on and off. Only works when the engine is not moving.
(8) PROTOCAST	Activates Proto-Cast which allows you to play music through the engine when an appropriate audio device is hooked up to the TIU.
(9) PFA	Activates Passenger/Freight Announcement sound sequence. One of the most popular features that was introduced by M.T.H. in 1996, has been improved upon in ProtoSound 2.0 with additional sounds helping to add even more realism to train stations or freight yards.
(0) DOPPLER	Activates Proto-Doppler, which simulates the Doppler effect sound. To function, this feature must be setup prior to use through the DCS Remote menus. Refer to the DCS User Manual for more information.
READ	Searches for TIUs, AIUs, and ProtoSound 2.0 engines on the track. You'll definitely want to do this after you add or replace engines on the track. This allows DCS to recognize the ProtoSound 2.0 engines and automatically place them in the Active Engine list on the DCS Remote.
E-STOP	Cuts power to all tracks controlled by DCS Remote. If you see an accident about to happen, press this button. I call this the safety net feature. I should note that even if your trains are traveling at high speed, they will come to a complete halt in a matter of a few inches. Once the E-STOP button is pressed you will need to reset DCS by powering down the Transformer and DCS Remote followed by turning them back on.

TIP:
You can vary the whistle/horn by pressing and holding the W/H button for 3 seconds or more. Doing so will cause different tone inflections in the ending of the whistle/horn sound ending depending on how long you hold the button down, producing a neat, varied effect.

Softkeys on the DCS Remote

Softkeys are a set of five keys labeled S1 – S5, located directly under the LCD on the DCS Remote. Unlike the One-Touch keys, these perform multiple functions depending on the item that is being operated, whether it be an engine, switch, or accessory – all right from the DCS Remote! This allows them to have a wide range of use, giving you a great amount of flexibility and control when operating your layout.

When operating ProtoSound 2.0 engines with the DCS Remote, you will see several groupings of three letters on the LCD just above the Softkeys. Each of the three letter sequences represents a different function

on the engine. Simply pressing the Softkey directly below it will activate that function. It is that simple!

After pressing the S5 Arrow Softkey twice, the S4 Softkey will show MORE. Pressing it will cause the LCD to show a complete list of all Softkey functions to choose from along with short descriptions of each.

As for the additional functions that the Softkeys can perform, you should notice that instead of letters above the S5 Softkey, there is an arrow that points to the right. When this Softkey is pressed, it serves to "scroll" to the right showing a new set of three letter functions under the S1 – S4 Softkeys giving you addi-

Below are some of the more popular Softkey codes and their descriptions. Keep in mind it is not a complete list. For more information please refer to the *DCS User Manual.*

SCS	Coupler Slack Sound
SI1 – SI8	Engine Idle Sounds (differs from engine to engine)
SFS	Forward Signal (two short whistle/horn blasts)
SRS	Reverse Signal (three short whistle/horn blasts)
S01 – S10	Various Engine Sounds (differs from engine to engine)
STW	Train Wreck Sounds
SSU	Extended Start-Up Sounds
SSD	Extended Shut-Down Sounds
SCC	Coupler Close Sounds
FMR	Measure Route (in scale miles)
DOD	Display Odometer (in scale miles)
DTO	Display Trip Odometer (in scale miles)

tional functions to choose from. Another press of the S5 Softkey will yield yet even more of the three letter functions.

At this point, you may wondering what all these stand for. Well, that is a good question and one option is to refer to the appendix of the *DCS User Manual,* which contains a list of the Softkey three letter codes that includes a description of their functions. Since this isn't always convenient, you may opt to continue pressing the S5 Softkey until the word MORE shows up above the S4 Softkey. Pressing the MORE (S4) Softkey will transform the LCD to show a menu in

which all the previous three letter functions are spelled-out. Using the thumbwheel on your DCS Remote, you can scroll up and down through the list of features. To choose the one you want, simply position the black triangle selector on the left side of the screen next to the function you want, and press down on the thumbwheel.

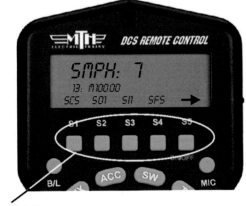

SOFT KEYS

The functions that Softkeys perform vary on the type of item that is currently being used.

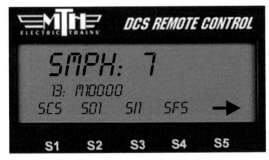

The arrow above the S5 Softkey allows you to scroll to another set of Softkey functions.

To help illustrate the power and flexibility of Softkeys, here's an operating example:
An ATSF 2437 SW-9 switch engine is idling on the track. You press the SCS (S1) Softkey. Then you scroll the thumbwheel up to start the switch engine forward and as soon as it start to move, you hear the Coupler Slack sound from the Softkey you just pressed. As the engine travels down the track, you decide you want it pull into a siding to pick up a hopper loaded full with coal. You push the SW button on your DCS Remote and scroll through the list of switches displayed on the LCD until find the one you want to change, pressing the thumbwheel to select the switch. On the LCD panel above the Softkeys you see a straight and curved set of arrows instead of letters. Simply pressing the corresponding Softkey will activate and change the switch to either straight or curved. Once your engine is in the siding and coupled up to the hopper, you decide it isn't quite full and needs more coal ... so you press the ACC button on your DCS Remote to show the list of accessories. You scroll through and choose the Coaling Tower (Item 30-9043). The Softkeys will now show the words ON, OFF, and ACT (for activate). Press the Softkeys to control the accessory. Note: I will discuss installing switches and accessories later in the chapter via an AIU.

OTHER DCS FUNCTIONS

Since DCS is chock-full of over 200 features, you will want to be sure to refer to the *DCS User Manual* for more information and instructions on those not covered in this chapter. I do, however, want to point out several excellent and innovative features included in DCS.

Feature	Description
Chuff Rate	ProtoSound 2.0 steam engines from M.T.H. come set from the factory with 2 chuffs per revolution of the drive wheels to accommodate operation in conventional mode. DCS allows you to change this setting to the more prototypical 4 chuffs per revolution to take advantage of the slow speed operation now capable in command mode.
Measure Route	The measure route allows you to measure a route on your layout in scale miles.
Setting Up A Route	For layouts with multiple switches and passing sidings, you can program a route for your train to travel. Activating a route will throw all the switches at once. You can even save routes to apply again during a later session.
Setting Up A Scene	Like setting up a route, you can set up a scene by activating a specific set of accessories you choose all at the same time.
Multiple Engine Lash-ups	Just like real railroads, you can string together several engines to pull that long freight train. Multiple engine lash-ups allow you to designate the lead, middle (if applicable), and end engines. Additionally, when you press the whistle/horn button on your DCS Remote, only the lead engine will activate.
Record/Playback an Operating Session	Just like a tape recorder, you store an entire operating session of up to 90 minutes or 500 button presses (whichever comes first) to be played back at a later time.
Odometer Readings	You can view both the current operating session and total odometer readings of ProtoSound 2.0 engines in scale miles with the DCS Remote.
Testing Track Signal	This feature allows you to test the signal strength coming through your tracks to your engine. It is a great tool to help identify dirty areas of track or places that need an additional electrical connection.

Clickity Clack Feature

The Clickity Clack feature is very fun – and realistic in how it imitates the sounds of wheels traveling over the joints between the rails of track. If you've ever stood by a passing train, you know what this sound is and M.T.H. has recreated it very well in this feature of DCS. To activate it, simply scroll the thumbwheel on the DCS remote up to any speed above 30 SMPH and leave it there for 30 seconds. If you adjust the speed, you will have to wait 30 more seconds before the Clickity Clack sounds begin. When they do, the engine sounds will dissipate. If it is a passenger train engine and you listen closely, you will hear the conductor asking passengers for tickets and a steward announcing that dinner is served. You'll even occasionally hear a passing train or the ringing sound of a crossing gate zipping by as well. To stop the Clickity Clack sounds, adjust the speed up or down and in a few seconds the regular engine sounds will return.

Operating in Conventional Mode

So far in this chapter, I have focused on setting up and operating ProtoSound 2.0 engines in command mode using DCS. One of the great aspects of DCS, however, is its ability to run all makes of trains from the oldest tinplate trains to the modern engines, allowing you to enjoy trains from all periods. In order to accommodate these types of trains, I will employ the use of the Variable Channel on the TIU. Don't worry, though, as this process will involve only a few modifications to the setup we already have in place on the Santa Fe Raton Pass Railroad. The really good news in this type of configuration is that you will be able to run your trains in conventional or command modes. You can even run both modes simultaneously if you choose!

Understanding the TIU Channels

The TIU comes equipped with a total of four channels – two Fixed and two Variable – with each channel having an IN and OUT. Upon close examination of the TIU, you will see a series of eight pairs of banana plugs; each pair has one black and one red plug. Four of the pairs along one side of the TIU represent the IN section while the four sets of plugs on the other side represent the OUT section. Above each pair of plugs there are labels identifying to which channel each set belongs. Before jumping in and reconfiguring the layout, it is important to know the difference between these two types of channels available on the TIU and what the characteristics are of each.

UNDERSTANDING THE TIU CHANNELS

Fixed Channel

These channels employ a constant amount of voltage coming from the transformer into the FIXED IN set of plugs of the TIU. Once inside the TIU, the digital signal of DCS is added to the voltage before it exits the FIXED OUT plugs, which lead to the track on the layout.

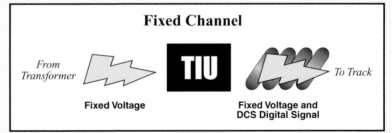

It is very important to note that the amount of voltage entering into the TIU is the same as the amount coming out of it. Therefore, the use of FIXED channels are generally reserved for command mode operation with ProtoSound 2.0 engines. You can run Lionel TMCC equipped engines in Command mode on this channel, but you will need to hook up your Lionel TMCC Command Base in conjunction with the TIU. I will explain how to do later on in this chapter.

Variable Channel

These channels also employ a constant amount of voltage coming from the transformer into the VARIABLE IN set of the plugs of the TIU. As with the Fixed channel, once inside the TIU, the digital signal of DCS is added to the voltage. However, this is where the similarities end. The resulting amount of voltage exiting out of the TIU through the VARIABLE OUT plugs and to the track is controlled via the DCS Remote. This output allows you to run your conventional style trains by raising and lowering the voltage, while still providing DCS signal to the track.

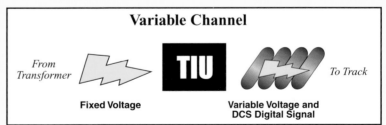

Since I only used one channel for the Santa Fe Raton Pass Railroad, you may be wondering why there are so many included on each TIU. The answer is two-fold: choice and expandability. Having two different types of channels allows operators a choice based on the type of model railroad equipment they own. On the flip-side, if model railroaders decide to expand by enlarging their layout with an additional loop or two of track, they are already prepared with the extra channels on the TIU. Those with larger layouts will find having these four channels available to be a necessity when distributing power evenly across the different tracks on their model railroads. And for those with very large layouts, having only four may seem limiting, but the good news is that you hook up additional TIUs to your layout and control them all with a single DCS Remote! For more information regarding this, please refer to the *DCS User Manual*.

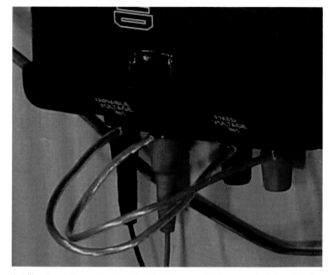

I utilized speaker wire to make the jumpers that connected the Fixed Voltage In1 and Variable Voltage In1. I made sure to match the red and black banana plugs respectively. The jumper wires provide power to the TIU when the Fixed 1 Channel is not used.

> **TIP:**
> Model railroaders with larger layouts that have multiple loops of track often designate one TIU channel per loop. This allows the user to simply press the TR (Track) button the DCS Remote to quickly change between the different channels, or loops of track connected to the TIU.

Wiring a Variable Channel on the TIU

Wiring a Variable channel on the Santa Fe Raton Pass Railroad is as simple as 1-2-3:

1. *Detach the wires connected to the **Fixed Voltage In1** plugs on the TIU, and reconnect them to the **Variable Voltage In1** plugs. Make sure to match the appropriate colored banana from the transformer to the **Variable Voltage In1** plugs on the TIU (i.e., red to red, black to black).*
2. *Detach the wires connected to the **Fixed (DCS) Out1** plugs on the TIU, and reconnect them to the **Variable (Conv/DCS) Out1** plugs, once again making sure to match the correct plugs.*
3. *In the previous setup using the Fixed channel, the TIU was able to draw power from that connection. Since that channel is no longer used, the TIU no longer is powered. To provide power to the TIU, you have two choices: plug a power source such as a M.T.H. Z-750 Transformer into the **Aux Power Input** plug on the TIU, or construct a set of jumper wires between the **Fixed Voltage In1** and **Variable Voltage In1** connections. On the Santa Fe Raton Pass Railroad, I chose to use the jumper wires. To do this, simply cut two short pieces of 16-gauge twisted pair wire. Take one of the wires and connect it from the red plug of the **Variable Voltage In1** to the red plug of the **Fixed Voltage In1**. Repeat this for the other wire using the black plugs for each of the inputs.*

Note: If you are adding a Variable channel while keeping the Fixed 1 channel connected, you do not need to install jumper wires as stated in step 3. As long as the Fixed 1 Channel is being used, the TIU will have power, so simply connect the additional wires from your transformer and track to the correct Variable plugs on the TIU.

Operating Trains with Variable Channels

As you'll recall, the main difference between Fixed and Variable channels is amount of voltage going to the track. Fixed channels send a constant amount of voltage to the track while Variable channels allow you to control the voltage. This difference will impact the way that trains operate on your layout when using a Variable channel. To see this difference, let me demonstrate how to control your trains in each mode of operation.

Conventional Mode

1. *Press the TR (Track) button on the DCS Remote. This will display the Track Menu on the LCD.*
2. *Use the thumbwheel to scroll to the track (TIU1 VAR1) and press to select.*
3. *The LCD will now show 0.0 VOLTS (instead of SMPH). Scroll the thumbwheel upward to increase the voltage to the track. You'll notice that the voltage jumps from 0.0 to 5.0 VOLTS immediately – this is normal.*
4. *Raise and lower the voltage using the thumbwheel to control your Conventional engines as you would normally do in that mode of operation.*

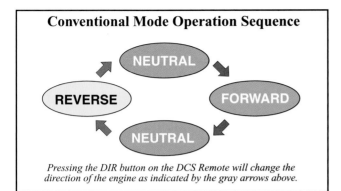

Conventional Mode Operation Sequence

Pressing the DIR button on the DCS Remote will change the direction of the engine as indicated by the gray arrows above.

One important difference between the Conventional and Command modes is the operational sequence. In Conventional mode, you begin in Neutral. The sequence then goes Neutral-Forward-Neutral-Reverse-Neutral-Forward.

> **TIP:**
> DCS allows the ability to rename your tracks for easier reference when selecting them with your DCS Remote. I did this on the Santa Fe Raton Pass Railroad, as I renamed the track TIU1 VAR1 to Raton Pass RR. See the DCS User Manual for more information on how to accomplish this.

Command Mode

When using the variable channel, the TIU adds the digital signal in with the voltage going to the track. Therefore, you can operate your ProtoSound 2.0 engines in command mode on a variable channel. Here are the steps to do this:

1. Press the TR (Track) button on the DCS Remote. This will display the Track Menu on the LCD.
2. Use the thumbwheel to scroll to the track (TIU1 VAR1) and press to select.
3. The LCD will now show 0.0 VOLTS (instead of SMPH). Scroll the thumbwheel upward to increase the voltage to the track until it reads between 16 and 18 volts.
4. Press the ENG (Engine) button on the DCS Remote.
5. Press the READ button on the DCS Remote. This will "look" to see what ProtoSound 2.0 engines are on the track and place them in the Active Engine List.
6. Use the thumbwheel to scroll to the engine from the list you want to control, and press to select it.
7. The LCD will now show the name of the engine along with 0 SMPH.

At this point, you can operate the engine as mentioned earlier in the chapter, and take advantage of all the great command mode features of DCS.

> **TIP:**
> Once the operation of trains in command mode using the variable channel is complete, be sure to power down the track voltage to zero before turning off the DCS Remote. In the event that you forget to do this, the next time you turn on the DCS Remote, it will remember the last voltage it was set at even though this may not match the actual voltage. When this happens, the DCS Remote and TIU are not in synch with one another. To correct this, simply power down the voltage on the DCS Remote and reapply it to the track to recalibrate the DCS Remote and TIU.

Both Modes at the Same Time

With DCS, it is possible to operate both command and conventional engines in their respective modes on the same track at the same time. To run trains of both modes at the same time, you will still have to raise and lower the voltage of the track. This will take care of the control of conventional engines. The key, though, is that even while the track voltage is going up and down, the digital signal of DCS is continuously being mixed in. As you will recall, command-equipped ProtoSound 2.0 engines will wait until they are ordered to perform an action. So as long as the voltage is up above roughly 8 or 9 volts, all you need to do is simply press the ENG (Engine) button on the DCS Remote, choose the ProtoSound 2.0 engine you want to control, and then start controlling it as you did earlier. To better illustrate this method, let me describe a sample operation session from the Santa Fe Raton Pass Railroad:

> I have two engines sitting on the track. One is a RailKing ATSF 4-6-4 Hudson steam engine with ProtoSound 2.0 (Command). The other is a RailKing ATSF NW-2 diesel switch engine with regular ProtoSounds (Conventional). On the DCS Remote, I press the TR (Track) button and select the *TIU1 VAR1* track. The LCD reads 0.0 VOLTS. Using the thumbwheel, I slowly dial up until it reads 11 volts and the NW-2 engine lights up with its diesel engine sounds beginning even though it stays in place. The Hudson steam engine is still dark and silent. I then press the DIR button and the NW-2 begins to move forward. Now I turn my attention to the Hudson steam engine by pressing the ENG (Engine) button on the DCS Remote, and select it from the list. With it on the LCD, I press the 3 (Start Up) button to initiate the engine's sounds and then slowly scroll the thumbwheel upward to increase the SMPH, which is what is now showing on the LCD. To switch back to control the NW-2 engine, I simply press the TR (Track) button and select the *TIU1 VAR1* track in order to raise or lower the voltage.

There are several drawbacks to this dual-mode operation of which you should be aware. First, when the DIR button is pushed, it resets the track to 0.0 volts. Not only do the conventional mode engines stop, but with no power, the command equipped ones are forced to as well. Secondly, when operating at lower voltages, command-equipped engines will not perform quite as smoothly. If you are just getting into model railroading using DCS, or are a seasoned veteran of the hobby, you may want to hold off on attempting this until you feel more comfortable with the system. Though this type of dual mode operation can be accomplished, it is more difficult than just operating in one or the other mode, as the user must think in "two modes" at the same time.

Accessory Interface Unit (AIU)

So far, I've shown you how to setup and run trains in the various modes using DCS. However, when a TIU is setup in conjunction with an AIU, you gain the ability to control nearly *everything* on your entire layout. The AIU is a series of relays that communicate with DCS to allow you to turn lights, switches, and accessories both on and off, as well as momentarily activate them with connections to control 10 accessories and 10 switches. If additional capacity is needed, the AIU is expandable by connecting another AIU to the existing one. This is referred to as daisy-chaining, and DCS allows up to five AIUs to be connected in this manner, *per* TIU. Five AIUs would enable the ability to control 100 different accessories and switches, which is probably more than most any layout would ever need. Keep in mind that additional TIUs can be added to the system and therefore create the potential—in conjunction with additional AIUs—to control up to 500 different accessories and switches!

Items Controlled by the AIU on the Santa Fe Raton Pass Railroad

4 Left Hand Switches

2 Right Hand Switches

Operating Track Section (Zia Lumber)

Operating Passenger Station Platform (Raton)

Operating Freight Station Platform (REA)

Operating Coaling Station (Morley Mine)

AIU Installation

Due to the large number of connections on the AIU (10 switches and 10 accessories), installation of the unit will take a bit of time; rest assured, it is a relatively easy and straightforward task. I began by making sure all of the existing DCS components were turned off on the Santa Fe Raton Pass Railroad layout. I then mounted the AIU on the component mounting wall underneath the layout right next to the TIU, fastening screws through each of the four mounting holes at each corner of the AIU to the component mounting wall. Next, using the included AIU/TIU cable, I plugged one end into the **TIU Input** port on the AIU, and the other end into the **AIU Input** port of the TIU. This cable provides communication between the two units. For the last step, I powered-up DCS and pressed the READ button on the DCS Remote. This only needs to be done after the initial installation of the AIU. Doing so allows DCS to automatically locate and map the AIU.

Wiring Accessories and Switches to an AIU

You'll first need to decide which items will be hooked up to the AIU, and which ones won't. Some accessories, such as the O Scale 3 Position Operating Semaphore, only need direct power from the transformer. For items such as these, I installed two additional M.T.H. Layout Wiring Terminal Blocks on the component mounting wall underneath the layout. I connected one to the 14 Volt Fixed Output, and the other to the 10 Volt Fixed Output on the Z-4000 Transformer, making sure to match the respective color of the banana plugs on each. I followed this by running 20-gauge wire from each item that needed power to the terminal block making sure to utilize the holes I drilled in the 1x4 cross supports of the train table. Doing so helped to keep the wires tucked up under the layout. One trick I employed here was to use color-coated wire with red for the + connections and black for the − connections; the wire can be purchased at most home improvement stores or at your local Radio Shack.

TIPS:
The 14 Volt Fixed Output and the 10 Volt Fixed Output on the Z-4000 Transformer gain power the moment the Z-4000 is turned on. You will want to keep this in mind when deciding which items you want to hook up to the AIU.

When wiring switches for use under DCS, do not use track power. Instead, a fixed voltage source such as the 10 volt or 14 volt connections on the Z-4000 Transformer is recommended. On the Santa Fe Raton Pass Railroad, I ran two wires (red and black) from each switch to a terminal block, and the remaining three to the AIU for control of the switch.

With all the accessories and switches wired for power, I then turned my attention to the AIU. Once again I ran the wires for these items underneath the layout to the AIU. For several of the accessories, I utilized 24-gauge rainbow wire. The rainbow wire I used contained four color coated wires held together by a thin, clear plastic sheath, and can be purchased at Radio Shack. It certainly helped to make the wiring process under the layout easier. On the side of the AIU, there is a series of wire connections for the accessories and switches: 10 are labeled ACC for Accessories, and 10 are labeled SW for Switches. These utilize small openings with a built-in screw on the top that, when tightened, hold the wire in place. Since these screws are very small, I used a flathead jeweler's screwdriver to perform this task.

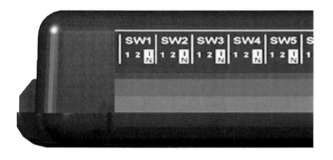

Each Accessory and Switch connection on the AIU contains three individual wire slots. Simply put a wire in the slot and use a jeweler's flathead screwdriver to tighten the built-in screw to hold the wire in place.

AIUs are very versatile as they can handle anywhere from two to five connection wires per accessory (switches usually have only three). Since accessories come in so many different configurations, you should carefully check the wiring instructions included with the accessory, as well as the *Accessory Interface Unit Operator's Manual*, which is included with the AIU. There you will find easy to follow wiring diagrams for the different number connections using sample M.T.H. accessories.

Setting Up Accessories and Switches in the DCS Remote

With the wiring of the accessories and switches to both a power source and the AIU complete, the next step involves setting them up on the DCS Remote.

1. *Make sure the Transformer and DCS Remote are turned on, and power transformer is set to 16-18 volts.*
2. *Press the MENU button on the DCS Remote.*
3. *Use the thumbwheel to scroll to SYSTEM and press to select.*

4. *Use the thumbwheel to scroll to either ACCESSORY SETUP or SWITCH SETUP and press to select.*
5. *Use the thumbwheel to scroll to either ADD ACCESSORY or ADD SWITCH and press to select*
6. *Use the thumbwheel to scroll to TIU number that the Accessory or Switch is connected to (via the AIU) and press to select. On the Santa Fe Raton Pass Railroad, I only used one TIU, so for each setup I chose 1 for this answer.*
7. *Use the thumbwheel to scroll to the AIU number that the Accessory or Switch is connected to and press to select. If you use more than one AIU daisy-chained together, simply count out from the TIU to get the AIU number. On the Santa Fe Raton Pass Railroad I only used one AIU, so for each setup I chose 1 for this answer.*

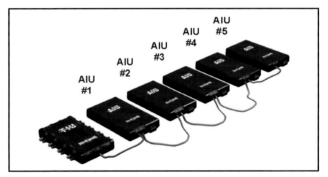

Each TIU can have up to five AIUs connected in succession (daisy-chained). The numbers indicate the address for each AIU which is needed when setting up accessories and switches in the DCS Remote.

8. *Use the thumbwheel to scroll to the AIU port (ACC1-ACC10 or SW1-SW10) that the Accessory or Switch is wired to, and press to select.*
9. *The LCD will display a list of letters and numbers. Name the Accessory or Switch by using the thumbwheel to scroll through the letters which will move a set of brackets [ ]. When the [ ] are around the letter you want, press the thumbwheel to select it. Repeat this process to select the letters, one by one, to make up the name of the Accessory or Switch.*
10. *To complete the naming of the Accessory or Switch, use the thumbwheel to scroll to the D at the end of the list and press to select. The Accessory or Switch is now named.*

TIPS:
If you make a mistake during the naming of an Accessory, Switch, or Engine, use the thumbwheel to scroll to the < character and press to select it. This serves as a backspace and will delete the mistake you made.

Instead of naming switches on the layout as "Switch 1, Switch 2," try giving them names that are specific to their location, such as "Gallinas Switch" or "Morley Siding." This will make it easier to recognize which switch is which when you bring up the list on the DCS Remote to activate them.

Controlling Accessories and Switches with the DCS Remote

Once the accessories and switches are setup on the DCS Remote, controlling them is very easy.

1. *Press the ACC (Accessories) or SW (Switch) button to access the respective menu*
2. *Use the thumbwheel to scroll through the list of available items, and press to select the one you want.*
3. *The LCD will now display the name of the item with the operational choices. Press the SoftKey under the LCD to select the choice you want such as ON, OFF, or ACT for Activate. The SoftKey choices for accessories will differ from those of switches.*

In previous years, the norm in the hobby was to create a large control panel that held not only the transformer, but also the controls to activate all the accessories and switches. With DCS, the need for the control panel is gone, as every item connected can be activated via the DCS Remote. And the best part is that you do these tasks *anywhere* around the layout.

TMCC and DCS

The other command mode system currently available in O gauge is the Lionel Trainmaster Command Control (TMCC) System. First announced in 1993, TMCC is quite archaic by today's technology standards, with its one-way communication to the engines and its very limited feature set. Even in light of these drastic design differences, M.T.H. engineers were able

to build TMCC compatibility into DCS during its development, creating the first universally compatible command control system in the history of O gauge. M.T.H.'s breakthrough allows hobbyists to control *all* of their trains with a single unit – the DCS Remote.

How DCS Works with TMCC

In order for DCS to operate TMCC engines in command mode, it employs the use of a TMCC Command Base. The process begins by the user giving a command via the DCS Remote, which in turn sends it to the TIU. The TIU translates the command into the TMCC protocol and forwards it to TMCC Command Base, where it is then simply relayed to the TMCC equipped engine to carry out the command.

Items Needed

To take advantage of this compatibility on the Santa Fe Raton Pass Railroad, there three items needed for the setup of TMCC with DCS. They include:
- M.T.H. TIU/TMCC Connector Cable (Item 50-1007)
- Lionel TMCC Command Base and power adapter
- 1 three-foot ength of 20-gauge wire

Installation

I began by mounting the TMCC Command Base on the left side of the component mounting wall underneath the layout table. I followed this by connecting the power adapter from the TMCC Command Base to an electrical outlet. Next, I took the TIU/TMCC Connector Cable and plugged the end marked "TIU" into the **Serial Interface (RS-232)** port

The near-complete setup of DCS components, wiring, transformer, and the TMCC Command Base. The only task left to do is connect the wires from the accessories and switches to the AIU.

on the TIU and the other end marked "TMCC" into the TMCC Command Base. Each end of the TIU/TMCC Connector Cable should have a small, white band with a label indicating which end it is. Lastly, I took the piece of 20-gauge wire and connected it from the black banana plug of the terminal **Variable (Conv/DCS) Out1** of the TIU to the **Ground Lead Connector** of the TMCC Command Base.

TIPS

The TIU/TMCC Connector Cable is uni-directional. Failure to match the plugs with the correct components will result in not being able to control TMCC equipped engines with DCS.

When using more than one channel of the TIU, run one wire from each channel's output-side black banana plug to the TMCC Command Base.

TMCC Equipped Engine Setup for DCS

To add a TMCC equipped engine to the DCS Remote follow these steps:
1. *Press the MENU button the DCS Remote.*
2. *Use the thumbwheel to scroll to SYSTEM and press to select.*
3. *Use the thumbwheel to scroll to ENGINE SETUP and press to select.*
4. *Use the thumbwheel to scroll to ADD ENGINE and press to select.*
5. *Use the thumbwheel to scroll to ADD TMCC ENGINE and press to select.*
6. *The LCD will display a list of letters and numbers. Name the TMCC engine by using the thumbwheel to scroll through the letters which will move a set of brackets [ ]. When the [ ] are around the letter you want press the thumbwheel to select it. Repeat this process to select the letters one by one to make up the name of the engine.*
7. *Use the thumbwheel to scroll to the number (1-99) that matches that specific engine's TMCC address on the TMCC Command Base and press to select. If you are unsure of this number or have not set one up for the engine, please refer to the* DCS User Manual *for more information.*
8. *Use the thumbwheel to scroll to the TIU that is connected to the TMCC Command Base and press to select. Note: If you are only using one TIU, select the first TIU in the list.*
9. *DCS adds the TMCC engine to the Inactive Engine List on the DCS Remote and assigns it an address number. Note: This number does not need to match the TMCC Command Base number.*

Operating TMCC Engines Using the DCS Remote

Once the TMCC equipped engine is setup on the DCS Remote, it can then be operated using the following steps:
1. *Press the ENG button on the DCS Remote*
2. *Use the thumbwheel to scroll down to the Inactive Engine List to locate the TMCC engine and press to select*

At this point, the TMCC engine will operate in the same manner as ProtoSound 2.0 engines by utilizing the thumbwheel to increase and decrease speed. Additionally, the One-Touch keys of the DCS Remote will operate the corresponding features on the TMCC engine. The TMCC features without a One-Touch key can be operated via the Softkeys area of the DCS Remote.

TIP:

The TMCC Cab-1 Remote Control can still be used, but will only be able to control the TMCC equipped engines. The Cab-1 and DCS Remote use different frequencies and will not interfere with one another.

The Future is Bright for DCS

M.T.H.'s introduction of DCS in April 2002 marked an important milestone in the hobby of O gauge model railroading. This revolutionary new system has uniquely blended today's technology with model railroading in a way never before seen or experienced by providing features that take realism to new heights. The great news is that it will only get better! With DCS being software-based, M.T.H. has provided a flexible system that is easily upgradeable. DCS will allow the hobbyists to keep their systems up-to-date by downloading new features and enhancements directly from M.T.H. via the Internet. This type of architecture means that the future of DCS is virtually unlimited. It is certainly not out of the realm of possibility that additions such as a personal computer control interface for a layout, as well as layout control via the Internet may be just over the horizon. Though we don't know exactly where DCS will lead the hobby, one thing is for certain – the future of O gauge model railroading has never been brighter.

Detailing Your
M.T.H. Layout

CHAPTER **9**

During the first several phases of constructing your M.T.H. Electric Trains layout, the focus was on major aspects such as the train table, laying track, building a divider, and creating mountains and other scenery. As you work toward completing your model railroad, you will get down to the smaller details such as buildings, roads, people, and signs.

What Are Details?

What exactly are "details" and how do they apply to a model railroad? In general terms, details are the smaller parts that make up a larger whole. For a model railroad, though, these details can take on a variety of shapes and forms. The best way to accomplish this facet of building your model railroad is by observing

real life – take careful note of objects and conditions found on and around real railroads. If the one you are modeling isn't close by, or is from earlier time, use the research you did earlier in Chapter 3. Videos, books, and magazines make excellent resources for you to draw upon for adding details to your model railroad.

Throughout this chapter, I will describe a variety of ways to add details to your layout by showing examples I incorporated into the Santa Fe Raton Pass Railroad. Several examples focus on creating new objects, while others deal with improving the appearance of those already in place. Whichever the case, the addition of these details can be an extremely fun and gratifying part of constructing your layout. The best part about it is that you can continue to add details to your model railroad long after it is done.

Weathering Structures

The buildings, stations, and industries on your model railroad are focal points for the observer. M.T.H. Electric Trains produces a wide variety of building structures that are pre-built and ready to place on your layout. Although they are finely detailed and pre-painted in realistic colors, they all come with that "new" look. To help make them even more realistic, I recommend that you employ a technique called weathering.

Use a wide tip brush such as this to apply chalk to weather your structures. You may even want to use your fingers to purposely smudge it to get the desired result.

Weathering makes a structure look like it is older by simulating the effects of nature's harsh elements, or years of neglect. One important tip to keep in mind is to vary the amount of weathering for different buildings on your layout since not all buildings in real life are in the same condition, or of the same age.

You can weather items as little or as much as you want, depending upon the kind of results you desire. I kept the weathering process very basic, using chalks and spray paint on the Santa Fe Raton Pass Railroad. Entire books have been written on this subject alone, and if you desire to do more, you can obtain one of the many books currently available.

I began with the chalks in variety of colors including black, gray, white, brown, and tan, from my local hobby shop. I used a small X-Acto knife to scrape the chalk to create a pile of powder on a piece of paper, and then applied the chalk directly to the building with a make-up brush. I spread the chalk dust out over an area, using my fingers to blend and purposely smudge the chalk. If I got too much or didn't like the way it looked, I simply used a damp cloth to wipe if off, and started over again.

Once satisfied with the results of the chalk, I applied some spray paint. (If this if the first time you've ever worked with spray paint, I suggest that you do a test with a scrap piece of plastic or wood to get the hang of it before attempting to weather a building that will end up on your model railroad layout.) Though many different colors and methods can be used, I used just two colors and applied the paint directly from the spray can. The first color I used was Floquil Grimy Black. Don't spray close to the building. Instead, you should think of this as more of an "over spray"; hold the can at least 18" away from the building and quickly move the spray can side to side. The goal is not to darken, but rather just get the structure a little "dirty." After each pass, stop and inspect your work. Since this paint is permanent, it is important to check that you don't apply too much. Once again, the general rule is to work from lighter to darker.

Using a very light spray of Grimy Black at distance on your structures and signals provides a nice "dirty" effect.

For chimneys and brick walls, you can use a product such as Modelers Mortar and Scenery Base.

A chimney with Modelers Mortar and Scenery Base applied. All it needs now is some black chalk to simulate ash and soot.

The next paint color isn't really a color – but provides excellent results in weathering your structures. It is Floquil Instant Weathering. No, thunderbolts and rain don't pour out of the spray can, but a kind of a tan/brown color paint that does an excellent job of simulating the effects of the elements of nature. Hold the can far away from the building when you spray. However, as you do, you will probably want to move the can closer in successive passes to achieve the result you want. As with the Grimy Black, work from lighter to darker when applying the Instant Weathering.

The last step in weathering your buildings and structures involves what I call "locking it in place." To do this, I used Testors Dull Cote, which is a clear, flat lacquer overcoat spray that will ensure that the paint and chalk will stay in place and not rub off.

Additional Ideas for Structures

Another great place to add detail is the chimney. You can simulate brick mortar a lot easier than you might imagine. First, remove the chimney – on most of the M.T.H. building structures, the chimney is held in place by a single screw under the roof. Then, you can use a specific mortar product, or use a basic white latex paint diluted with a little water. In either case, all that is needed is to wipe it on with a cloth, making sure it fills in the crevices. Follow this by wiping the excess off with a damp cloth and then allow it to dry. The coloring should remain in the crevices where the mortar belongs. As for the inner part of the chimney, simply paint the inside black to simulate soot buildup from smoke.

One of the more subtle details on your layout involves the height of building structures, such as passenger stations and industry buildings, relative to the track. Since M.T.H. RealTrax comes with the built-in roadbed, your trains will sit well above the surface of the train table. Thus, the respective heights of the train and the station platform will not quite match, causing that last step off the train for the passengers to be a real "lu-lu." To rectify this situation, I suggest using 1/4" foam board or corrugated cardboard to raise the structures up to the appropriate height. On the Santa

Fe Raton Pass Railroad, I placed foam board underneath all of the building structures (with the exception of the switch tower in Trinidad).

Improving Building Fronts

The Buildings Unlimited Building Fronts come molded in the colors of red and gray. Though they look fine as they are, you will probably want to paint them to achieve greater realism for your town. On the Santa Fe Raton Pass Railroad, my father-in-law used a small brush to hand paint almost all of the building fronts using a variety of colors. As you can see, the results are outstanding.

Another way to improve the look of building fronts is to add backgrounds you place directly behind them. These can be purchased from Buildings Unlimited to simulate the inside of stores on the bottom level and rooms, complete with curtains on the upper levels. The addition of these backgrounds adds depth to the building, helping to produce a three-dimensional look.

For the building fronts that don't have corresponding backgrounds, add window shades. Place several small pieces of masking tape on the back side over the window. Be sure to only cover 1/4 to 3/4 of the window, varying this amount from window to window. Cover the remainder of the window with black paper. Viewed from the front, you'll see a nice depth-adding effect.

Trackside Details

The area adjacent to the railroad track is referred to as the "right-of-way," and is an excellent place to add details to your model railroad layout. Items such as oil spots right on the track (using glossy black paint), to the placement of a piece of rail (painted brown) off to the side, to weeds and tall grasses growing parallel to the tracks, all aid in producing a varied and realistic look.

Without the foamboard under the station platform, there is a big last step off the train.

Adding the foamboard closes the distance between the step and platform, making it more realistic.

Signals

M.T.H. produces an excellent line of O Scale signals that have been a real hit with consumers. When used in conjunction with an Infrared Track Action Devis (ITAD), they simulate realistic operation from corossing gates lowering to lights changing color in sequence. I incorporated several of these signals on the Santa Fe Raton Pass Railroad, which not only look good, but added a lot of action to the railroad.

As good as the signals are, you may want to enhance their appearance to accentuate their realism. You can do this by applying a very a light spray of Floquil Grimy Black to weather them. The key is to keep this very light, as your goal should be to make them look just a little bit dirty. You can also apply Testors Dull Cote to the signals, which takes away their shine and glossiness.

Consider enhancing your signals to match the research you did on the particular railroad you are modeling. I did this on the Santa Fe Raton Pass Railroad in two particular ways. First, the Cantilevered Signal Bridge was originally silver. Since the Santa Fe doesn't have any silver signal bridges on Raton Pass, I painted it black to match those that do actually exist in that location. Secondly, upon close observation of several train videos, I modified the Semaphore Signal to match those on the Santa Fe. M.T.H.'s Semaphore originally came with the arm painted mostly yellow and a pointed tip at the end. I simply cut the tip off with a pair of pliers to create a straight edge, and painted it black. I then added a small yellow stripe near the end.

A mixture of black- and rust-colored chalk produced this nice looking effect on the side Trinity Transport Company.

Details, such as oil spots on the track, an extra rail painted brown, various weeds and other growth, will greatly enhance the right-of-way on your model railroad.

Roads and Crossings

There are several techniques you can use to improve your roads and crossings. Using a black pen or pencil, you can draw lines for cracks on streets, curbs, and sidewalks. Don't forget to add a few potholes on the streets for that extra-special touch. Another technique you can employ involves putting dark dots on the timbers of your railroad crossing to simulate the bolts that hold them in place in real life. Lastly, the application of gray and/or black

I modified this semaphore signal to match those I saw on videos of the Santa Fe.

This was originally a silver cantilevered signal bridge. I painted it black to match the signal bridge on the real Raton Pass.

Applying Testors Dull Cote to signals removes their original gloss and shine.

chalk powder to your roads will create the effect of lanes where vehicles traverse as well as making the roads look a little older and well traveled.

Signs and Billboards

Adding signs and billboards to your layout not only lends an air of authenticity, but also give a sense of place to different locations on your model railroad. I personally found this particular aspect of adding details to the layout to be a lot of fun; there are so many ways to produce excellent results.

I used several of the Woodland Scenics Dry Transfer Decals throughout the Santa Fe Raton Pass Railroad layout. The great part about these decals is how easy they are to apply. I simply cut them out from the sheet, placed them face down where I wanted to apply the decal, used a pencil to rub the backside of the paper, and then pulled the paper off leaving the decal in place. I used the decals in a variety of places including many windows on the building fronts, and on an old wooden fence near the Zia Lumber Company in Raton.

I created many of my own signs using my home computer. With advent of color printers, easy-to-use software, and free clipart graphics on the Internet, even a novice can create some great-looking graphics.

Adding chalk to your roads simulates age as well as lanes where vehicles travel.

Two Woodland Scenics Dry Transfer decals make excellent additions to the old fence.

In the town of Trinidad on the Santa Fe Raton Pass Railroad, I had a large brick wall with no windows facing one of the sidings. I printed several billboards on regular paper and then glued them directly to the wall. I then weathered the wall to give them the well-worn look, producing a nice focal point for the observer.

I had a lot of fun with the theater in Raton. I did a search on the Internet for actual theaters in Raton, New Mexico and found the El Raton. Since I wanted a railroad theme movie to be playing, I chose the 1946 hit movie *The Harvey Girls* starring Judy Garland. (This movie also happens to be where the Oscar-winning song *On the Atchison, Topeka, and Santa Fe* came from.) I used my computer to make the marquee signs and did another search for an original movie poster on the Internet. Using a graphics software application, I shrank the picture and printed two copies off, placing them in the "Now Showing" windows next to the

doors of the theater.

I chose to make my own decals for several signs on the Santa Fe Raton Pass Railroad. Walthers makes 8-1/2" by 11" sheets of clear decal paper, which you can feed, carefully, through your laser printer. To apply the decals that you create, cut them out of the sheet then dip them in a bowl of water for 30 seconds. Next, very carefully slide the decal film off the paper onto your structure in the proper place. You'll have a few moments to move the decal into position – I find that a pair of tweezers and a wet Q-Tip work best for this. Decals are quite fragile and can tear, so be sure to handle them with care. Once properly positioned, allow the decal to dry.

Scenic Elements

Though we previously discussed the construction of realistic scenery, you can still add certain scenic elements to help in detailing your model railroad. Bushes and weeds around buildings help to create the illusion

To match the actual town of Raton, I placed a sign on the top of the mountain.

Signs along the track give a sense of place to your model railroad.

Adding billboards, such as these printed on my home computer and then weathered, turn an ordinary wall into a focal point.

*The El Raton theater looks complete with a movie about the Santa Fe Railway. A search on **www.mapquest.com** provided the real street names on the signs I added to the M.T.H. Operating Traffic Light Set (30-1089-1).*

The decals on the stations and switch tower were made using Walther's Decal Paper.

When adding trees, don't forget to add some Woodland Scenics Dead Fall to simulate broken branches and dead trees on the ground.

that the structure has been there a while. Another way you can add scenic elements to your layout is with Woodland Scenics Dead Fall to simulate broken branches lying on the ground. These pieces can be placed at the base of trees, on mountains, or even in streams and rivers.

People and Vehicles

Without people, there wouldn't be much of a town – or railroad, for that matter, so remember to add these important details to your layout. M.T.H., and several other companies, produces a wide variety of different figure sets. In fact, M.T.H. even makes one with people in sitting position for the interior of your passenger cars.

Though the figures are pre-painted, I suggest giving them a wash of black acrylic enamel diluted with water (4 parts water, 1 part black paint). Simply brush it on the figures and use a paper towel to wipe off the excess. The dark coloring should seep into the indentations and crevices, bringing out facial features more vividly and sometimes even the wrinkles on the clothing! When placing the people on the layout, you can put several together to tell a story or create a mini-scene of activity.

Placing realistic vehicles is another important facet of your model railroad. Strategically placed, these can add impact and realism to your layout. But just as in real life, some vehicles should be clean and shiny, while others should be dirty. Be sure to use some Instant Weathering paint on several of the vehicles you place on the layout.

The more details you add to your layout, the more realistic appearance it will take on. And the great part is that you can continue to add details well after the main part of the layout is completed, so you can keep it fresh and exciting.

Adding people and vehicles help to create mini-scenes that tell a story.

The Dispatcher Game

As you have seen throughout the course of this book, building a model railroad layout with M.T.H. Electric Trains is a very entertaining and rewarding endeavor. With all this fun, you may be thinking that it can't get any better ... but it can! In order to get even more out of your model railroading experience and avoid the possible burnout from the constant repetition of running your trains in circles, try playing *The Dispatcher Game*.

The Dispatcher Game challenges you to operate your trains in a way that real railroads do, giving an important sense of purpose to every action of each train all the way on down to an individual piece of rolling stock. The game combines purpose with the imagination of the players involved to provide a much more enjoyable experience of running your M.T.H. Electric Trains. *The Dispatcher Game* is an excellent individual game, as well as one that allows for the involvement of others – such as family and friends – to use teamwork and communication to achieve a common goal. Lastly, it's a great tool for learning more about real railroads, and how and why they operate the way they do. The best part, though, is that you can play this game on any layout, big or small, and still have lots of fun.

The Premise of the Game

The premise of *The Dispatcher Game* calls for players to simulate the actions of a railroad in real life. Up until this point, you have focused on researching, planning, and building a realistic model railroad with the installation of the state-of-the-art technology found in Digital Command System (DCS). Now it is time to take it all a step further by turning your layout into a miniature transportation system through the realistic movement of freight and passengers. The truly great part is that, in utilizing many of the terrific features of DCS, it will seem as though you are the engineer inside your M.T.H. locomotive! You'll find that, unlike video games, *The Dispatcher Game* involves true three-dimensional interaction – allowing you to experience O gauge model railroading like never before.

Since real railroads are large and complicated, you obviously won't be able to fully emulate their actions. However, with a little imagination and a few innovative tricks, you can create your very own railroad empire that will provide hours upon hours of excitement – long after you have completed the construction of your layout.

To make things a bit easier, *The Dispatcher Game* is broken down into three levels: Brakeman (Beginner), Conductor (Intermediate), and Engineer (Advanced). So, if you've never attempted realistic operation with your trains, try each level.

Before You Get Started ...

Structure of Your Layout

In order to gain the full benefit from *The Dispatcher Game*, there are several points to consider before you begin. The first point concerns the structure and design of your layout. Hopefully, back in Chapter 3, you added plenty of sidings and industries along the mainline for your railroad to serve. If you did, you'll have numerous switching options, which in turn will give you many different operating combinations. But if you didn't, don't fret: there are a few tricks that will help you if you only have a siding or two on your layout.

The Era of Operation

Another item to consider are the various eras of railroading. To help you achieve the greatest level of realism, be sure to run the trains that existed and operated in a given era. For example, an F-3 diesel would be appropriate to run alongside a 4-6-4 Hudson steam engine to recreate the Transition Era.

Name Every Location

Since one of the key features in *The Dispatcher Game* is the movement of freight and passengers, it is vitally important that you name every location on your layout. You can mimic the real railroad you are modeling when you assign names, or you can make up your own names. The illustration from the Santa Fe Raton Pass Railroad shows that I used a variety of location names that do exist around to the towns of Raton and Trinidad. Although in reality many of these locations are miles apart, they must be collapsed into a smaller area in model railroading.

You'll note on the illustration that all of the switches on the Santa Fe Raton Pass Railroad are named. The good news in this part of the process is that you probably named your switches when you set up your DCS, so you will just need to go a bit further and name all the other items on your layout.

Naming locations and clearly marking them will give a sense of place, and allow you to easily reference trains by their location.

Location	Description
Switches (or Turnouts)	Not only will naming every switch make it easier when operating them via your DCS Remote, but also make it easier to reference a location marker for your trains when you are operating them. For example, it is easier to recognize the "Gallinas Switch" on the DCS Remote's LCD screen than "Switch 4."
Towns	In most instances, a town will be where a station is located and have the same name. However, you can also name locations along the rail, such as a large curve or a group of buildings, after a town. I did this on the Santa Fe Raton Pass Railroad: a MTH Operating Water Tower represents the town of Starkville.
Scenic Areas	Name passes, canyons, mountains, rivers, and lakes. These natural points of reference add realism on your layout.
Industries	Industries are generally thought of as buildings and factories located next to sidings. However, they can also include coal mines, quarries, fuel depots, lumberyards, and freight stations. Industries are very important when playing *The Dispatcher Game*, as freight cars will be delivered to and from them – so be sure to name as many of them as you can.
Yards	Yards come in many shapes and sizes and perform a variety of duties. However, most yards serve to sort and classify freight cars in order for them to be delivered or returned to a final destination. If your yard is large enough, you may want to name certain areas and tracks within it for points of reference when switching trains and cars around.
Interchanges	Much traffic on any given railroad comes from other railroads, and interchanges are the points in which two railroads connect. Often one railroad will set out several freight cars on this track for the other railroad to pick up and deliver to their final destination. An Interchange on your layout can be as simple as a siding, or even part of the mainline, and can play a key role in providing freight car traffic – especially for smaller model railroad layouts limited by space.
Team Tracks	Team Tracks are a shared siding. Usually, these sidings are out in the open without any buildings next to them. Freight cars are left on the track to be unloaded onto trucks for delivery to various companies; this practice allows the railroad to serve several "industries" on one track and is another good trick to utilize on smaller layouts if possible.

Double-Name Industries and Locations

If your layout is already built and you don't have many industries, try a technique I call "double-naming." Double-naming involves giving two different names to one location on your layout. For example, some of the time an industry building along a siding may be the "Moreno Valley Meatpacking Company" and later on it may be the "Kuchenbecker Furniture Warehouse." Double-naming allows you to increase the number of "places" on your layout without adding a building or structure, providing more places for your freight cars to travel among.

Making Your Layout Bigger than It Really Is

One of the limitations of model railroading is the edge of the train table: No more room and that's it, right? Well, not exactly. A trick to make your layout seem much larger than it really is involves a bit of "thinking outside the box" – or, in this case, thinking outside the train table. You can create "virtual" locations just off the edge of your model railroad for freight car and passenger train destinations. Some examples include: A large town or city, intermodal train yard, or a big industry complex such as an oil

Double-naming an industry is an excellent idea to increase the number of "locations" on your layout. One building can serve as two different "locations," giving your railroad freight cars to deliver.

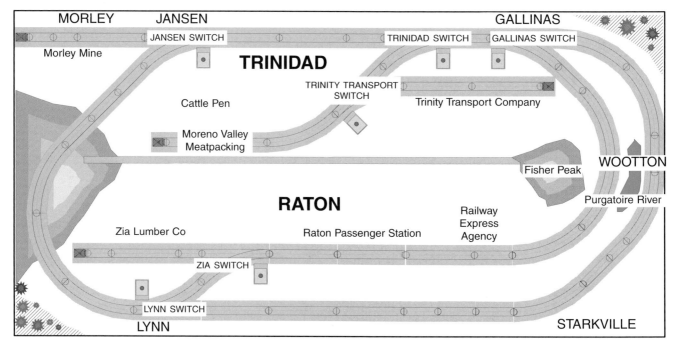

In addition to naming locations on the Santa Fe Raton Pass Railroad, I also gave names to the switches. This not only gives a sense of place, but doing so also helps when referencing them using DCS.

refinery. Though the physical size of the layout stayed the same, you just increased its "virtual" size tremendously as your trains now have much longer distances to travel and more places to go.

Slow Down Those Trains

In years past, O gauge engines had only three speeds: stop, fast, and very fast – all fun, but not very realistic. One of the hobby's best innovations is the DCS Handheld's ability to display scale miles per hour on the LCD screen, allowing your M.T.H. Electric Trains to creep along at very slow speeds. Imagine your steam engine chuffing along at 5 scale miles per hour with labored, synchronized smoke churning from its stack; it's a sight worth seeing!

Keep in mind that different trains travel at different speeds. For example, a hotshot passenger train runs much faster than a freight train of hoppers fully loaded with coal. So, depending upon the scenario, try slowing your freight and passenger trains down to realistic speeds.

Personal Modification and Flexibility

Last, but not least, among the things to consider before you begin, is that you can modify this game to suit your individual tastes. It is a game for you, and it is designed for fun, so if there is a certain aspect you don't like, or something just doesn't seem to work well on your railroad, go ahead and cut it out. Being flexible in this way will allow you to get the most enjoyment out of the game that you possibly can.

Beginning the Game ...

Brakeman (Beginner)

One of the goals of *The Dispatcher Game* is to operate your model railroad much like a real one. Size limitations require that we take a few liberties, and make some adjustments, while letting our imagination fill in the rest. The first step is to get your trains organized, and make sure that the engines and cars that you plan to use are ready to use. A good-sized yard is the ideal place to put the trains you plan to use for this game. But if your space is limited (like mine is on the Santa Fe Raton Pass Railroad), you will need to place and remove trains from the tracks periodically during the course of the game. A good location for these excess trains is the storage shelf below the layout. Storing them there makes them easy to get to, and keeps them safely out of the way.

Next, create a simple Train List showing the trains you plan to run during the course of the game. This list can either be handwritten on paper, or done on a computer as shown from the example of the Santa Fe Raton Pass Railroad. Your Train List is your guide for *The Dispatcher Game*, so keep it handy, as it holds key information about what trains you will run, where they will go, and what they will do. Your Train List, coupled with the great features of DCS, puts you in complete control of your railroad.

To help describe the Brakeman Operating Session, I have broken down the Train List by numbered areas to describe the activities of the game.

❶ *Knowledge of your own railroad, whether through research or made-up information, will come in handy at this stage of the game. Providing a name, district, division, and subdivision help give the Train List a definite sense of place and purpose. Since I chose to create the Train List for the Santa Fe Raton Pass Railroad on a spreadsheet program, I was easily able to insert the Santa Fe logo for authenticity – and you may want to do likewise for your own Train Lists. If you plan to operate during a specific era or time, you may want to include the date for a touch of realism.*

❷ *This area of the Train List deals with the Type and Name of the train, along with several other pieces of important information. The Type is simply whether it is a Freight or Passenger train. The Name area shows the specific name of the train or its function, along with a brief description. All long distance Passenger or Freight trains have origination and destination towns which help with our idea of having trains appearing in one place and traveling to another location – both exist somewhere off the outer edges of the layout, which not only makes the layout seem larger, but also greatly increases operational possibilities and gives you a much greater number of towns and cities for your railroad to "interact" with. Lastly, a priority grade is assigned to each train. Generally, Passenger and Fast/Express Freights are given High priority, while other Freights and Locals will be relegated to Medium and Low grades.*

❸ *Here's where you will list the motive power involved in the train. On the Santa Fe Raton Pass Railroad, I chose to put the road name down because a locomotive from another railroad occasionally is "borrowed" by the Santa Fe to pull a train. I also put down the number that is on the engine itself, as well as the type of diesel or wheel arrangement, if it is a steam locomotive. Here's a tip: Make this the same as the name on your DCS Handheld for easy reference when operating your trains (which will probably involve changing the name on your DCS Handheld, or using the original Smart-Read name from the DCS Handheld).*

Santa Fe Railway
Northern District
New Mexico Division ❶
Raton Subdivision

Date: 5/15/1952

E   Clockwise
W   Counter-clockwise ❹

Train List

Type	Name	Motive Power	Laps	Train Schedule
Freight ❷	Express Refrigerator Cars *High Priority*	ATSF 2926 4-8-4	E 7 6 4	Start at Trinidad ❺ Stop at Raton for crew change Stop at Starkville for water End at Gallinas
Passenger	Superchief Chicago to Los Angeles *High Priority*	ATSF 16 F3	W 3 12 8 8	Start at Wootton Stop at Trinidad PFA Stop at Raton PFA ❻ Stop at Jansen PFA End at Lynn
Freight	Local Deliver Freight Cars *Low Priority*	ATSF 2437 SW9	W 3 5 2 3	Start at Raton ❼ Stop at Wootton for train passing Stop at Trinidad deliver car to Trinity Transport Stop at Raton pickup car at Railway Express Agency End at Jansen
Freight	Through Mixed Consist Argentine to San Bernardino ❸ *Medium Priority*	ATSF 960 4-6-4	W 9 15 5	Start at Raton Stop at Starkville for water Stop at Lynn for train passing End at Wootton

Beginner (Brakeman) level train list.

❹ The Santa Fe Raton Pass Railroad is built upon the basic loop layout design, which allows for operation in either direction. If this is the case with your model railroad, you can incorporate the use of direction in your train list. To do so, simply assign East to all clockwise direction trains and West to all that travel counter-clockwise around the layout (though you may choose to use North and South depending on your railroad). Running trains in alternate directions promotes the perception that trains are coming and going just as they do on real railroads.

❺ The Train Schedule area is truly the heart of the Train List – it specifically catalogs each action that the trains will perform. To begin, place the engine listed, along with its respective cars, on the track at the assigned location on the layout, being sure to adhere to the direction listed in the Laps column. If your layout is large enough to contain a yard, you may want to originate most or all of your trains from there. Next, using your DCS Handheld, operate your train around the layout the number of times noted in the Laps column. During this procedure you can activate many of the great features of DCS, such as Proto-Doppler and Clickity-Clack Sounds, as well activating those great sounding whistles and horns on your M.T.H. engines. Follow the indicators on your M.T.H. O scale signals such as the Operating Semaphore and Cantilevered Signal Bridge by going a bit slower or stopping altogether if they show a yellow or red signal. Once your train completes the number of laps listed, stop it at the location listed in the Train Schedule column. You may want to wait a few moments and listen to the realistic Cab-Chatter of the crew from your M.T.H. locomotive while you do. Then start your train and follow the same steps in completing laps arriving at the next destination, repeating this process until you finish the operation of that specific train. When the End notation is reached, the train effectively "leaves" the layout toward its final destination. At this point, remove the train from the layout and replace it with the next train on the Train List. Keep in mind that if your layout is small, use higher numbers of laps (as I did with the Santa Fe Raton Pass Railroad), while larger layouts will require smaller numbers of laps.

❻ When operating a passenger train on your Train List, you'll want to be sure to take advantage of the Passenger Station Announcements feature in ProtoSounds by simply pressing the PFA (Passenger/Freight Announcements) button on your DCS Handheld. This ultra-realistic rendition of the arrival announcement of the train, followed by sound sequence of passengers getting off, is a favorite of many hobbyists. You can utilize this feature at each stop listed in the Train Schedule column. You'll also notice on the sample listed above that the Superchief is scheduled to stop at several locations that don't have a passenger station. Instead of doing this, you may opt to use the passenger station at Raton each time, incorporating the Proto-Dispatch feature of DCS by speaking into the microphone on your DCS Handheld while pressing the MIC button. This way, each stop at the station can be announced as a different town, thus making the layout seem much larger. This is great trick, especially for those with smaller layouts. Don't forget that if you have an M.T.H. Operating Station Platform, you will be able to activate it with your DCS Remote to simulate people getting on or off the train.

❼ Probably the most fun and challenging aspect of operating your M.T.H. Electric Trains in accordance to the Train List is delivering to, and picking up individual (or groups of) freight cars from various industries. You will be able to activate the Proto-Couplers on your M.T.H. engine to pick-up and drop-off cars anywhere on the layout without the use of a special uncoupling track. The sample Train List notes that one of the actions involves the delivery of a boxcar to the Trinity Transport Company. The illustration sequence shows how to accomplish this feat. You'll note that when the train arrives in Trinidad, there is a refrigerated car at the Moreno Valley Meatpacking Company. In order to deliver the boxcar, the refrigerated car ("reefer" for short) must be moved out onto the mainline temporarily. This allows the engine with the boxcar to travel up the siding past the Trinity Transport Switch. After the switch is thrown via the DCS Handheld, the engine will then back the boxcar into the Trinity Transport siding for delivery, using the Proto-Coupler to release it. After the engine returns to the mainline, it will then proceed to return the reefer car back to the Moreno Valley Meatpacking Company before continuing on to the next town. Whenever uncoupling needs to take place in the middle of the train, employ "Mr. Hand, Your Personal Brakeman" (your other hand that is not holding the DCS Handheld). Using one of your fingers, you can easily flip down the small tab on the side of the coupler to open and release the coupler. Likewise, if you have difficulty getting two cars coupled, your Personal Brakeman can also help in this area. Just be sure that Mr. Hand doesn't move any cars around – considered cheating! – since part of the challenge of the game is to make your M.T.H. switch engine to do all the work, just as an actual switch engine does on a real railroad.

TRINITY TRANSPORT SWITCHING SEQUENCE

Whistle/Horn	Description
o	Stop, or apply brakes.
— —	Start, release brakes.
— o — OR —	Approaching stations or junctions.
— — o — OR — — o o	Approaching road crossing at grade.
— o o o	Trainman protect rear of train.
o o o o o	Warning to people or animals to get off the track.
o o o	If stopped, the engine is about to back up. If the engine is running down the track, it means the train will stop at the next station.

o = Short Toot; — = Long Toot.

Utilize Realistic Horn and Whistle Signaling

For optimum fun with *The Dispatcher Game*, include proper whistle and horn signals. Railroads use such signals as a language of sorts, and you can do likewise when operating your M.T.H. Electric Trains. The table above lists a few of the many signals employed by railroads.

Multiple Train Operation

Once you feel comfortable operating your railroad using a Train List, you may want the added challenge of multiple train operation. Running two or more trains at the same time is easy to do with the DCS, and adds a twist to *The Dispatcher Game*. You can run both trains yourself, or you can invite a friend or family member to join in on the fun using additional DCS Remotes, putting each person in charge of a different train. Whatever the case, you'll want to make use of the Priority notation for each train on the Train List. Inevitably, two trains will meet at some point on your layout. The train with the higher priority will take precedence – meaning that the lower priority train needs to move to a siding to allow the higher priority train to go by first. If both trains are running the same direction, the lower priority train will need to "move over" to allow the other one to pass it.

Reusable Train Lists

Creating a Train List for *The Dispatcher Game* will take some planning and preparation time up front. However, I think you will soon see that the rewards of operating your M.T.H. Electric Trains in this manner far outweigh the time you put into creating your Train Lists. To help save on prep time, preserve your Train Lists for another operating session of *The Dispatcher Game* later. After several lists are made, you'll find you have a stack from which to choose (shuffle the stack every so often to avoid repetition).

Conductor (Intermediate)

The next level of *The Dispatcher Game* involves the addition of several pieces of information to the Train List. These additions are designed to replicate real railroad operations, as well as add a bit more of a challenge to operating your M.T.H. Electric Trains. Several new terms and features of the game are added to this level. Below is an example of the Conductor Level Train List.

❶ *You may notice that the Type column has been replaced with the Class column. Real railroads categorize their trains into different classes. The table shows these different classes.*

❷ *A caboose, listed by the number on its side, is added here in the Motive Power column. If you double- or triple-head engines together, list each engine here in order of appearance on the train.*

❸ *The notation of a Helper Engine is listed here. The Santa Fe Railway often required the use of additional locomotives to help trains pull their loads up the steep grades of Raton Pass. Simulate this action by creating a lash-up of two ProtoSound 2.0 engines in command mode using the DCS Handheld as shown. After several laps, representing* The Chief *traveling over the pass, uncouple the helper engine and pull it on a siding track, allowing* The Chief *to continue without it.*

❹ *Additional designations for Local trains are added in the Name column. Two particular types are Turns and Sweepers; a Turn is a local that begins in one location, travels out to perform switching duties, and then returns to its starting location. (Turns are typically named after their location preceding the word Turn; i.e., Raton Turn.)*

Sweepers are generally local trains that travel to the various industries on the route and pick up freight cars.

❺ *This level introduces the Train Order, which is a separate sheet expanding upon the Train Schedule column in the Train List.*

Santa Fe Railway
Northern District
New Mexico Division
Raton Subdivision

Date: 6/17/1952

E   Clockwise
W   Counter-clockwise

Train List

Class	Name	Motive Power	Laps	Train Schedule
Second **❶**	Express Refrigerator Cars Bakersfield to Chicago	ATSF 2920 4-8-4 Caboose: 1910 **❷**	E 7 6 4	Start at Trinidad Stop at Raton for crew change Stop at Starkville for water End at Gallinas
First	Superchief Los Angeles to Chicago	ATSF 17 F-3	E 3 12 8 8	Start at Wootton Stop at Trinidad PFA Stop at Raton PFA Stop at Jansen PFA End at Lynn
Fourth	Local Deliver/Pickup Freight Cars Train Order #12 **❺**	ATSF 2437 SW-9 Caboose: 999600	W	Start at Raton *See Train Order for Detailed Instructions*
Third	Through Mixed Consist San Bernardino to Corwith	ATSF 3700 4-8-2 Caboose: 999471	E 9 15 5	Start at Raton Stop at Starkville for water Stop at Lynn for train passing End at Wootton
First	The Chief Chicago to Los Angeles	ATSF 11 E-3 ATSF 960 4-6-4 (H) **❸**	W 8 5 14 10 9	Start at Trinidad Stop at Lynn PFA Stop at Raton add Helper engine Stop at Jansen uncouple Helper engine Stop at Gallinas PFA End at Starkville PFA
Third	Through Hoppers - Coal	N&W 2160 Y6b Caboose: 1997	E 5 7 6 4	Start at Raton Stop at Lynn for train passing Stop at Starkville for water Stop at Trinidad for crew change End at Gallinas
Fourth	Local - Sweeper **❹** Pickup Freight Cars Train Order #13	ATSF 2419 NW-2 Caboose: 1604	W	Start at Raton *See Train Order for Detailed Instructions*

Conductor (Intermediate) level train list.

CLASSES OF TRAINS

Class	Description
First Class Passenger Service	Both limited and local passenger trains.
Second Class Fast Freight and Express	Non-stop except for crew changes, refueling, and icing for refrigerated cars.
Second Class Manifest or Through	Service between yards, drops off blocks of cars to be delivered to local industries.
Third or Fourth Class Locals	Does local switching in small areas, also delivers cars left by other trains.
Extras	Not on schedule, usually designated with prefix of Extra before the name. They can include both passenger and freight trains, as well as non-regular Maintenance of Way and Troop Trains.

Santa Fe Railway
Northern District
New Mexico Division
Raton Subdivision

Date: 8/17/1952

(1) **Train Order #12**

Crew Name: Rusty A. and Bob K.
Engine: ATSF 2437 SW-9
Train Name: Local - Raton to Starkville
Direction: Westbound

(2)

Switch List

Depart RATON				
Proceed 8 laps **(3)**				
MORLEY				
Morley Mine	Deliver	ATSF	181764	HOPPER - EMPTY
Proceed 3 laps				
TRINIDAD				
Moreno Valley Meatpacking	Pickup	ARLX	8008	REEFER
Trinity Transport Company **(4)**	Deliver	ATSF	142472	BOXCAR
Proceed 5 laps				
LYNN				
Zia Lumber Company	Deliver	WP	13206	LOG CAR - LOADED
Proceed 7 laps				
GALLINAS				
Wait for passing train **(5)**				
Proceed 2 laps				
RATON				
Railway Express Agency **(6)**	Deliver	ATSF	48216	BOXCAR
Proceed 4 laps				
JANSEN				
Cattle Pen	Deliver	ATSF	128016	STOCK CAR
Proceed 5 laps				
Arrive STARKVILLE **(7)**				

Sample train order.

Train Order and Switch List

Switching freight cars to and from industries on your model railroad can provide some of the most fun, challenging, and rewarding experiences in the operation of your M.T.H. Electric Trains. To elaborate on the actions found in the Train Schedule in the Brakeman Level of *The Dispatcher Game*, the creation of a Train Order with a Switch List has been added. A sample is shown below:

❶ *Train Orders used on real railroads have individual, sequential numbers to identify them, and the ones used in* The Dispatcher Game *follow this convention. The overall structure of our Train*

Orders *has been modified to fit the premise of the game, though, and is utilized only with local freight trains. Keep in mind that, like Train Lists, you can re-use Train Orders again in another instance of the game.*

❷ *Crew, Engine, Train Name, and Direction are all included in this area of the Train Order. The Crew information can be made up or follow the actual name of the operator, while the other information should match what already exists on the Train List.*

❸ *Under the Switch List area of the Train Order, the first action to take place is the departure of the train. Note the engine and cars needed for the* train, and place them on the tracks followed by starting up the engine. Once all signals are clear, the train departs from that location, completing the number of laps listed.

❹ As with the prior Brakeman Level of the game, perform switching moves to pickup and deliver freight cars to various industries. The big difference here, though, is that each freight car is specifically identified, giving a bit of added complexity to the movement. In operating this way, you face challenges similar to those real railroad engineers do when delivering and picking up cars. For extra fun, initiate the Freight Yard Sounds sequence by pressing the PFA button on your DCS Handheld.

❺ The Zia Lumber Company has an automatic track section on the siding for dumping logs (used in combination with an operating log car) using the DCS Handheld. All of the freight cars listed in the Train Order are noted by their four- (or sometimes less) letter call name and number that is on the actual car itself. It is important to note that the number on the M.T.H. freight car doesn't match its catalog product number.

❻ On the Santa Fe Raton Pass Railroad, I used an M.T.H. Operating Freight Platform for the Railway Express Agency location next to the Raton Station. This not only allows me to deliver and pick-up freight cars, but to activate the Freight Platform with the DCS Handheld as well. Seeing a load of freight sitting on the platform before a boxcar arrives, followed by it "leaving" when the boxcar is loaded and picked-up, is quite a sight, providing an extra sense of realism.

❼ The end of the Train Order is marked by the arrival of the train at its final destination. Upon completion, you will manually remove the train from the tracks and continue on to the operation of the next train noted on the Train List.

Engineer (Advanced)

The Engineer Level of The Dispatcher Game is designed specifically for a larger layout due to aspects such as multiple train operation, multiple operators, and longer train consists. For the illustrations in playing this level of The Dispatcher Game, I will refer to the track layout diagram of Tom Grimason's model railroad, as shown below.

As indicated by the different colored track, Tom's layout has two levels. Additionally, Tom has built a roundhouse for his engines and allowed for several yards and sidings, which provide much greater operational capability and flexibility when playing The Dispatcher Game.

Yards and Multiple Train Operation

This aspect of the game involves assembling freight trains in a yard and sending them out around the layout. Set up the first train by using a small diesel or steam switch engine to put together the train consist on a main or secondary track. With the DCS Handheld you will be able to utilize the Proto-Couplers on your M.T.H. engines, along with "Mr. Hand," if necessary, to complete this task. Creating a train in this matter is a lot of fun, as you'll quickly find yourself turning into a true Yard Boss.

Once the train is assembled, hook up the engine(s) listed in the Motive Power column of the Train List and move out. Be sure to utilize the Coupler Slack Sounds from the Soft-Key area of your DCS

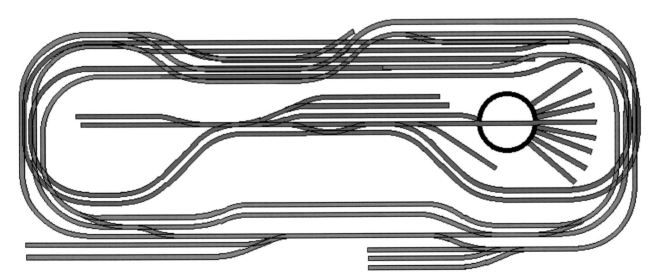

Tom Grimason's Union Pacific Model Railroad Layout. The two colors represent the different levels on his layout.

Santa Fe Railway	Date: 5/19/1952
Train Manifest	
Type: Through	
Class: Third	

| From: | Corwith | To: | San Bernardino |

| MOTIVE POWER: | ATSF 2920 4-8-4 | CABOOSE: 999471 |

Car		Type	Contents
ATSF	48216	BOXCAR	Glassware
ATSF	12873	BOXCAR	Empty
DRG	64119	BOXCAR	Appliances
ATSF	166593	GONDOLA	Scrap
TCX	878991	TANK	Petroleum Oil
DRG	22718	FLAT	Steel Pipe
ATSF	95932	FLAT	Lumber
ATSF	142472	BOXCAR	Furniture
CB&Q	83105	GONDOLA	Steel Coils
ATSF	13448	REEFER	Frozen Meats
SEPX	8124	TANK	Gasoline
ROCK	500700	COVERED HOPPER	Grain
ARLX	8008	REEFER	Beer
ATSF	26425	STOCK	Cattle
ATSF	37691	BOXCAR	Empty

Sample train manifest.

Handheld, as well as the Labored Chuff/Diesel Rev feature as you do. This would also be an opportune time to employ the route feature of the DCS to preset all the switches in advance of the train.

With DCS's scale-mile-per-hour increments, set the freight train to travel at a slow crawl, causing it to take a while to make it all the way around your layout. In the meantime, you can assemble the next freight train, following the same steps as before, but with the goal of trying to get the second freight out and going before the first one makes it around again. Depending on the size of your layout, you may be able to make up more than two trains and get them running at the same time.

Once you have made several trains in the yard and have them all out on the mainline, you'll want to have one of them "arrive" back at the yard. If you only have one yard on your layout, you may want to double-name it so that one physical location can serve as two differently named places. In this way, your train can travel from one "yard" to another "yard" even though it is the same physical location on your layout. The neat part is that this point-to-point travel is how most trains on railroads in real life operate.

Train Manifests

To help organize the freight train consists, use Train Manifests – listings of the engine(s) and all the freight cars in a particular train. Using a Train Manifest will provide order and clarity when assembling freight trains in the yard. Again, the creation of these will take some time up front, but you can use them again in other operating sessions. A sample Train Manifest is shown above.

Adding a Passenger Train

After mastering multiple freight train operation, you may want the added challenge of introducing a hotshot passenger train to the mix. Since passenger trains are of a higher class than freights, they travel faster and have priority over the freight trains. Thus, the task of managing trains passing one another over the course of your layout will take some fast reactions and quick thinking, just like a real dispatcher, in order to keep all those trains running smoothly on your model railroad!

Multiple Operators

Adding multiple operators is another option in playing the Engineer Level of *The Dispatcher Game* (you should note that multiple operators can be utilized in any level of the game). Multiple operators can be utilized in any level of the Dispatcher Game. It provides the perfect opportunity to share the great hobby of model railroading with friends and family members, as well as promoting teamwork and cooperation to achieve the common goal of keeping trains running.

When playing *The Dispatcher Game* with multiple operators, each person should have their own DCS Handheld. If your friends have DCSs, just tell them to bring them along when they come over. Since the DCS Handhelds can read multiple TIUs, your friends can be up and running trains on your layout quickly with their own DCS Handhelds. (The first time they do visit, they will need to go through the setup, and add the locomotive engines on the layout.)

With multiple operators, you will be able to split up duties on your railroad by having each person assigned to different tasks. For an example, one person can be responsible for making up freight trains in the yard, while another person can operate the trains once they leave the yard. Working together on your model railroad layout in this way is not only a lot of fun, but the time spent together can help to develop deeper relationships, and a sense of camaraderie among friends and family who participate in *The Dispatcher Game*.

A True 3-D Interactive Game

Through participating and playing *The Dispatcher Game*, every train operates with a specific purpose, and each action has importance. This not only provides a challenge, but makes operating your M.T.H. Electric Trains fun, exciting, and different almost every time. When combined with the state-of-the-art technology found in the DCS, your M.T.H. Electric Trains literally come alive with features never before experienced in the hobby, leaving you feeling as though you are inside the cab of a real railroad engine. Not only that, but *The Dispatcher Game* affords the opportunity to share the hobby with family members and friends, making it a truly interactive, family-oriented game.

A Dream Layout –
Tony Lash's
Spectacular M.T.H.
Layout

CHAPTER 11

Photo courtesy of M.T.H. Electric Trains

Interview with Tony Lash

Tony Lash is an avid model railroader and strong supporter of M.T.H. Electric Trains. His breath-taking 70-by-45-foot layout is a prime example of the trend in recent years toward much great realism in O gauge. The following is an interview with the remarkable man behind the layout. Tony tells of his past, discusses his layout, gives his opinions on the hobby, and ponders the future of model railroading in O gauge.

Rob: What early experiences in your life caused you to develop an interest in trains?

Tony: Well, when I was about five or six years old, I saw a Lionel operating layout in a department store and it was very intriguing. Also, my grandfather worked for the Norfolk & Western Railway, so trains were a part of my life ever since I can remember – probably about three years old. On a daily basis, my grandmother used to take me down to the East End Shops in Roanoke, Virginia, to take my grandfather his lunch. And there were always trains and steam engines all over the place, and it was always fascinating to see. That's what got me interested in trains.

Rob: When and how did you get involved in the hobby of model railroading?

Tony: I got my first electric train set in 1947. I was seven years old at the time, and I guess that was the beginning of my involvement in the hobby.

Rob: What kind of train set was it?

Tony: It was a Lionel train set and it was "6" something – 634 or something like that – I don't remember offhand. Anyhow, it had a little operating coal car with a red V-shaped body that dumped coal when it tilted to the side. It also had a Sunoco tank car, hopper, a brown B&O boxcar, a brown Lionel caboose, and there was, I believe, a little white refrigerator car.

Rob: You left O Gauge for a while and then you decided to get back into O Gauge. When did you get back into O Gauge, and what prompted your return?

Tony: I guess I was about 15 when I left the train hobby. And, quite naturally, seeing as I was a young man, I took up the hobby of young ladies. All my trains were packed away at my mother's home. I came to Washington, D.C., from Roanoke to get a job, and then I got called to the Vietnam War. After I got back from the war, I got married and we had our first child.

Back in about 1970 or 1971 – our boy was about three years old, I believe – we had bought a house and it was time to introduce him to electric trains. So I went home to Virginia and got all my old electric trains, and set up a new layout back in about 1970 or 1971.

Rob: What was the first M.T.H. item that you ever bought?

Tony: The first M.T.H. item that I ever bought was the Premier Norfolk & Western Y6b locomotive in 1994 or 1995 – my first M.T.H. engine.

Rob: Why did you buy that particular item? What interested you besides the historical connection to your childhood?

Tony: Well, I saw a brochure at a local hobby shop and it was the first articulated engine that I had ever seen for O gauge railroads, and I also discovered that M.T.H. was located right here in Maryland. I went over to take a look at it, and I was so intrigued and so impressed with the M.T.H. engine that I bought it right on the spot. And, I have loved it ever since!

Rob: And you still love it today?

Tony: I still love it today.

Photo by Rob Adelman

Photo by Rob Adelman

Rob: Would you say it is still your most favorite engine in your collection?

Tony: Yes, I would say that Y6b would be my most prized engine.

Rob: It's well known that you are a strong supporter of M.T.H.. Why are you such a strong supporter of M.T.H. Electric Trains today?

Tony: Well, I'm a strong supporter of M.T.H. because when I first got back into trains in the early 1970s, there was just nothing out there for you to buy. A lot of people get on me when I say it was junk, but it was! I bought a lot of the MPC boxcars that would just fall apart and the couplers and the trucks would, you know, wouldn't stay coupled and so forth and so on. They had some beautiful paint jobs back then, but the engines and things like that just wouldn't run good – it just didn't have the quality. Also, Lionel was charging high prices for this stuff.

So, when I just happened to run across that M.T.H. brochure that I mentioned earlier, it just looked like everything was top quality. I saw roadnames that I had yearned for, but which had never been done by Lionel. I just drooled at seeing these things. There were also articulated engines and cabooses with all kinds of roadnames. With M.T.H., I could buy a variety of rolling stock in all kinds of roadnames, including a

wide assortment of passenger cars. M.T.H. started producing items that people longed for, and had been asking Lionel for years to build. But Lionel just turned a deaf ear to these requests. So, this is what made me fall in love with M.T.H.. First was the quality, and second was the variety.

Rob: When did you decide that you wanted to build a realistic O gauge train layout, and why?

Tony: I had been a long-time reader of *Model Railroader* and several other scale modeling magazines. I could see all of the beautiful detail on the models in those publications, and I had gotten to the point where I was just tired of the toy look. You know, the coal loader, the barrel loader, the coal ramp – all of those were great Lionel accessories. But, it came to a point where there just wasn't enough realism for me, and I was looking for the type of realism I would see in the magazines and on other people's layouts.

I had built several other layouts before I built my current one, and I didn't care how I ran the track or what track pattern I had. No matter what I did, it just didn't look real. It still looked like a toy even if you added streets, sidewalks, and telephone poles. It didn't look like a real operating railroad. I wanted to operate a railroad in a prototypical way, and be able to switch out boxcars, drop off a car, work in the yard, and this, that, and the other. Even with good track plans using

Photo by Rob Adelman

Photo by Rob Adelman

Lionel track, those earlier layouts just didn't look real. I just couldn't get the desire for more realism out from inside of me. I've always said, from as far back as 20 or 30 years ago, that if I ever got to the position that I could build a real scale-looking railroad, but using three-rail track, I would just love it.

At one point, I had started to go into two-rail scale modeling. But I visited a lot of two-rail layouts and they always seemed to have some kind of electrical problem, or you couldn't walk into a hobby shop and easily find items that you needed, such as switches and things like that. Also, a lot of two-rail people had to hand-lay their track and switches, and that just wasn't for me. So, I wanted something that looked real but that still used three-rail track. Anyhow, after years of hard work building my business, the day came when I was able to build my dream layout.

Rob: Could you elaborate a bit on the evolution of your outstanding layout? Like, when did you start the planning process; when did you start construction; and when did you get it finished?

Tony: Well, when we moved the company to this location in Capitol Heights, Maryland, I found that I had this big, open room that we didn't really need for our business activities. We bought eight acres here, with three buildings and the main office building on the land. I just didn't need all of that space for my business operations. So, having a room this size available was really a big first step in making my dream layout come true.

Once I decided to build the layout, I proceeded to draw my own track plans, and so forth and so on. When I was satisfied with my plan, I hired Vernon Peacher, from Custom Model Railroads/Custom Model Bench Work, out of Hood, Virginia, to construct the benchwork. He came up and measured the room. I showed him my track plans and he drafted a blueprint; showed me how everything would work; and gave me a price for building the benchwork.

Vernon built the entire supporting structure and did all of the track work according to my plan. It took about eight months to do all the benchwork, which was done in sections – just like a modular layout. Vernon put everything together in his Virginia shop and had me drive down to look at it. We made a few changes and then the layout was shipped to its new home in Maryland. When it was finally put together, it fit into this room just like a glove!

From that point on, I had a lot of people come in and help me because I never could have built this layout by myself – not in my whole lifetime, even if I spent 10-12 hours a day working on it. So, I got people who

Photo by Rob Adelman

were experts in their fields to apply their skills.

One of these individuals was Bill Fosbrook, the electrician. He wired every light, and installed lights in the buildings and everywhere else they were needed.

Then I called in different people with different skills and talents to do the scenery and buildings, and things like that. It took about another year and a half with about eight or nine different groups of people at various intervals to develop this layout to the point where it is today. Sometimes these crews worked for weeks. Sometimes we had a crew that would just work on the weekend. They would come in on Friday and would work straight through until early Monday morning. We did that on a number of weekends. That's basically how this layout came together. Overall, it took us about three years to get to this stage.

Rob: What do you enjoy most about your layout?

Tony: I most enjoy sitting here just watching it run and knowing that I am able to operate it. I built it so I wouldn't need five people to help me operate it. I built it so I could operate my layout all by myself, and not have to wait on my buddies to come over so everybody would have a section to run. I get a lot of enjoyment out of just running it by myself, and sometimes I just want to come in and just work over in the coal yard. Just switching trains out, or making up trains here, or in this yard over here. Sometimes I just want to come in and run passenger trains – you know, whatever fits the mood that I'm in at the time. Other times I may want to run a lot of freights, and that also provides a whole lot of enjoyment. It's a challenge being able to run four trains at one time – two of them on each loop. Moving them from one loop to another by working the signals and avoiding accidents really makes you think, and requires you to always be alert. You know, it keeps my mind sharp! It's one of the things I use to keep me from getting old!

Rob: That's great. What are your plans for the layout's future? Do you plan to expand it even more? Are there any changes that you would like to make?

Tony: Well, I hope one day to retire, and I'm hoping to possibly move all of this to my

home when I sell my business. I live on a ten-acre site out in Fairfax, Virginia, and was thinking of putting up a room there that would be maybe 150 feet by 75 feet.

I did make some mistakes with this layout that I would correct if I do another one. I have some passing sidings that will easily accommodate 15-car trains, but when you start double-heading and triple-heading today's large steam locomotive models that are each some 30" long and that can easily pull 50 or 60 cars, even these long sidings are far too short.

I also wish I had put in a three-track main line where I could, for example, run passenger trains in the middle and freights on the two outside lines, or whatever. I would like to expand it to provide for several large yard areas, including a double-ended yard so trains could enter and exit from both ends.

I would also like to have a passenger station that is not just a dead-end terminal. You know, a run-through type of arrangement so trains would not have to back into or out of the station.

Overall, though, there's very little on this layout that I would change. The few changes I mentioned would make it even more enjoyable, but I really can enjoy this layout just the way it is. You know, you never get finished building a layout. There's always something else to do. For example, the manufacturers came out with some great ore hopper cars, and now you want a 50-foot long steel mill to justify their existence on your layout. That's a bit of an exaggeration, but you know what I mean. Right now, though, I'm happy with what

Photo by Rob Adelman

Photo by Rob Adelman

tially make DCS the number one operating system in the hobby. Now, it's always possible that five years from now somebody else or some other manufacturer will come out with something. But, right now, and I would say that in the next five to ten years, I think DCS will, based on what I have seen, be the main operating system for O gauge electric trains.

Rob: What other things do you see in the future of the O gauge hobby?

Tony: Well, it's kind of sad, because I don't see children in hobby shops buying trains. I visit a lot of hobby shops, from New York all down through North Carolina, and out west to Ohio. Wherever I go, and no matter what town I'm in, I always stop at the area hobby shops. I talk to a lot of shop owners and from what I have seen and heard, it's the 45- to 75-year-old guys who are in the hobby shops spending their dollars. I don't see the 22- to 25-year-old crowd, and I don't even see the thirty-something things.

When I started back in the hobby, my son was the main reason that I came back, and M.T.H. was the main product that attracted me. Today I just don't see the younger generation sharing that same sort of view. They are more intrigued with all of the computer gizmos and games and so forth.

I'm not going to say that the hobby will completely die out, of course, because a person can get hooked on the train hobby, even if he is 40 or 50 years old, or even older. But people just aren't exposed to the trains today like they were years ago. When I was growing up, department stores, hardware stores, and even five-and-dime stores like F. W. Woolworth had trains, and maybe even a train layout. Everybody – every kind of store – had a train layout. Everybody, it seems, sold Lionel, American Flyer, and Marx – even some drug stores.

But this was before the age of shopping malls. These days, malls dominate the retail-shopping scene, and space in mall stores is very expensive. You'll find very few mall stores that can afford to devote space to a train layout. And, since there are no layouts, kids don't ever get a chance to see trains run. Sure, they may

I have. If I don't do anything else to this layout, I still will be very content.

Rob: How do you think the new Digital Command System (DCS) from M.T.H. will impact the O gauge hobby?

Tony: I think it will have a great impact on this hobby. As you know, M.T.H. has tested DCS on my layout. I guess I'm part of the problem relating to why it's not out at this point because when I would have a question or find something not quite right, I would report it to M.T.H.. They would then to go back to the drawing board to see what could be done.

DCS is such a versatile and expandable system that it does take some time to get everything just right. There are some future capabilities of the system that I'm not at liberty to talk about right now, but DCS will offer things to model railroaders that they have not even dreamed about to this point. People will be asking, "What else could I possibly want it to do?"

You know, some 20 or so years ago, people probably asked that same question about the latest TV, VCR, tape recorder, or some similar object that was available back then. And look at what we have today! So, DCS will offer features that today's hobbyist hasn't even thought about yet. And all of these things will make the hobby more interesting because your trains will be even more prototypical in terms of what they do and how they operate.

There are a number of other things that would poten-

walk by a hobby shop and see a little train running around in a window, but that's about it. You don't see any kind of detailed layout with coal loaders running, Ferris wheels circling, log loaders doing their thing, and so forth. So, I think the hobby is in real trouble unless there are some other ways of introducing the hobby to kids. I think that Hi-Railers all across the country – the folks who are building beautifully detailed O gauge layouts and modules – are doing a magnificent job by setting up in malls on holidays and things like this to try and get kids interested. But that's just not enough. The hobby needs to be seen in the Wal-Mart, Target, and Kmart kinds of stores where so many people do their shopping. Ideally, there should be layouts for people to operate, view the accessories in action, and that sort of thing.

Rob: Andy Edleman, Vice-President of Marketing at M.T.H., has spoken about the hope that all of the features of the DCS control system and the new technology that's included in the system will draw more kids into the hobby. Do you share that view?

Tony: Yeah, I share the same view. Of course, Andy can talk about some things that I can't talk about because he is inside the company and can speak for the company. I have to be careful about talking about what I may know, because I don't want to step on anyone's toes, or discuss future things that are not yet announced. Still, I know there are a lot of new and exciting things that will be offered by DCS, and these things will appeal to kids as well as adults.

But I still think that kids have got to see an operating layout if they are going to develop any sort of interest in DCS or any type of model train. The parents need to see these things in action, as well. After all, how often does the typical parent visit a hobby shop these days, unless someone in the family is already involved in a hobby of some sort? Normally, they will go to Toys-R-Us, Wal-Mart, or some other such place to buy toys and hobby-type supplies, and they almost never see trains promoted and sold at those places.

My own feeling is that manufacturers really need to take a more active role in promoting the hobby and exposing it to kids and the public in general – particularly during the holiday shopping season – just like Lionel did so well in the old days. For example, manufacturer-sponsored layouts and displays in the open hallway areas at malls would be great. If there's a hobby shop in the mall, maybe the manufacturer could assist by providing some money so the shop owner can rent some additional space just outside his store. I think that would certainly be a more effective use of advertising money. People see ads in magazines and then put them down and move on to something

Photo courtesy of M.T.H. Electric Trains

Photo courtesy of M.T.H. Electric Trains

Photo by Rob Adelman

Photo by Rob Adelman

Photo by Rob Adelman

else. If they see trains up and running on a layout, they're far more likely to be motivated to buy something.

And, I think it would be a good idea for members of the various train clubs, both local and national, to have fund raisers from time to time to help to sponsor more public displays like this during the holidays. Think about it: Even if there's a hobby shop in a particular mall, only a small percentage of the mall's patrons go into that store. However, if there's a display out in one of the public hallway areas, it's likely that nearly all of the shoppers will see it at some point. People – young and old alike – need to see these trains in action to fully appreciate the potential of this hobby.

Rob: Last question. What advice would you give to a person who is just entering the O gauge hobby?

Tony: I would say it's a wonderful hobby and it's a family-orientated hobby. I would recommend that they go to *O Gauge Railroading* magazine's forum on the Internet and ask a whole lot of questions. You have a lot of intelligent people participating there, and that's the best advice that I could really give. I think newcomers need to be able to go to an Internet forum

and be able to ask all kinds of questions before they jump in with both feet because it can be an expensive hobby – especially if you are a collector and an operator.

But this is not a hobby where you have to spend $20,000 to have fun. Getting started really isn't all that expensive. For around $200 you can get a complete starter set that will get you going. For $500 or $600 you can buy a decent starter set, some extra track and switches, the DCS control components, and a sheet or two of plywood. That's really all you need to get going in a big way.

It's a great hobby! All that's needed is to take that first step!

Model Railroad Reference Resources for O gauge

Magazines

Classic Toy Trains
21027 Crossroads Cir.
P.O. Box 1612
Waukesha, WI 53187
www.classtrain.com

O Gauge Railroading
P.O. Box 239
Nazareth, PA 18064
www.ogaugerr.com

Internet Resources

M.T.H. Electric Trains Web site
www.mth-railking.com
One of the leading Web sites in the industry, it is full of easy-to-navigate information and resources such as:

- Dealer locator – find an M.T.H. dealer near you.
- Product locator – search through a database of dealer inventories from around the United States and Canada to find that item you've been looking for.
- Shipping schedule – stay up to date on when the latest M.T.H. products will be hitting dealer shelves.
- Newsletter – sign-up for an online newsletter that is delivered directly to your   e-mail inbox to keep up with the latest from M.T.H..
- Catalogs – view either the latest catalog or past ones right online in the popular PDF file format.
- My M.T.H. – create a wish list of M.T.H. items that friends and family can view right online. You can also track your train collection as well as check your free mthtrains.com e-mail account. And coming soon you will be able to have Personal Digital Assistant capability to consult your collection track while at hobby shops and trains shows.
- MTHRRC – special area available to M.T.H. Railroader Club Members complete with message boards and sneak peaks at new product offerings.
- Parts – should you need a replacement part, you can order it directly online. On select products you can also view exploded parts diagrams right on your computer.
- Service – allows you to search for an authorized M.T.H. Service Center near you or arrange for your item to be sent directly back to M.T.H. for repairs. With a Return Authorization number you receive, you can track your repair and see exactly when it is completed.
- Video clips – not sure how to lubricate your new M.T.H. engine? Instructional videos will walk you through the process of many regular maintenance procedures as well as demonstrating new features and product releases.

O Gauge Railroading Forum
www.ogaugerr.com/forum.html
Read and post comments regarding model railroading in O gauge.

Third-Party Products

BackDrop Warehouse
P.O. Box 27877
Salt Lake City, UT 84127
www.backdropwarehouse.com
Makers of scenic murals and backdrops for all scales.

RR-Track by R&S Enterprises
P.O. Box 643
Jonestown, PA 17038
www.rrtrack.com/rrtrack
Layout design software included on the M.T.H. RailWare CD ROM.

Woodland Scenics
P.O. Box 98
Linn Creek, MO 65052
www.woodlandscenics.com
Provides a full line of terrain and scenery products for model railroading.

Organizations and Clubs

M.T.H. Railroaders Club (MTHRRC)
7020 Columbia Gateway Dr.
Columbia, MD 21046
www.mth-railking.com
E-mail: club@mth-railking.com
Bring the excitement of M.T.H. Electric Trains home through a variety of membership benefits such as:
- Limited Edition Club Car.
- *The CrossingGate®* club magazine.
- First Class mailings of M.T.H. catalogs.
- Access to the MTHRRC portion of the M.T.H. Web site.
- RailWare® Software CD-ROM.
- Special club merchandise.
- Club card and lapel pin.

HiRailers Unlimited
10433 Shadyside Ln.
Cincinnati, OH 45249
www.hirailers.com

Toy Train Operating Society (TTOS)
25 W. Walnut St., Ste. 308
Pasadena, CA 91103
www.ttos.org

Train Collectors Association (TCA)
National Business Office
P.O. Box 248
Dept. 10
Strasburg, PA 17579
www.traincollectors.org

American Steam Locomotive Wheel Arrangements, Whyte Classification System
www.steamlocomotive.com

APPENDIX 2

Wheels	Whyte System	Name
OO	0-4-0	4 Wheel Switcher
OOO	0-6-0	6 Wheel Switcher
OOOO	0-8-0	8 Wheel Switcher
oOOO	2-6-0	Mogul
oOOOo	2-6-2	Prairie
oOOOO	2-8-0	Consolidation
oOOOOo	2-8-2	Mikado
oOOOOoo	2-8-4	Berkshire
oOOOOO	2-10-0	Decapod
oOOOOOo	2-10-2	Santa Fe
oOOOOOoo	2-10-4	Texas
ooOO	4-4-0	American
ooOOo	4-4-2	Atlantic
ooOOO	4-6-0	Ten Wheeler
ooOOOo	4-6-2	Pacific
ooOOOoo	4-6-4	Hudson
ooOOOO	4-8-0	Twelve Wheeler
ooOOOOo	4-8-2	Mountain or Mohawk
ooOOOOoo	4-8-4	Northern
ooOOOOO	4-10-0	Mastodon
ooOOOOOOo	4-12-2	Union Pacific
ooOOO OOOooo	2-6-6-6	Allegheny
ooOOOO OOOOoo	2-8-8-4	Yellowstone
ooOOO OOOoo	4-6-6-4	Challenger
ooOOOO OOOOoo	4-8-8-4	Big Boy
oOOOO OOOO OOOOo	2-8-8-8-2	Triplex

M.T.H. Electric Trains Item List for the Santa Fe Raton Pass Railroad

M.T.H. RealTrax

Quantity	Item #	Description
12	40-1001	10" Straight Track
11	40-1002 O-31	Curved Track Section
2	40-1004 O-31	Right-hand Switch
4	40-1005 O-31	Left-hand Switch
1	40-1008	Operating Track Section
10	40-1012	5.5" Straight
3	40-1016	5.0" Straight Track
5	40-1018	3.5" Straight Track
4	40-1024	Lighted Bumper
7	45-1028	O Scale ITAD Signal Box

M.T.H. Accessories

Quantity	Item #	Description
1	30-1062	O Lamp Set (Hexagonal)
1	30-1087	Road Sign Set
1	30-1088	Telephone Pole Set
1	30-1089-1	Operating Traffic Light Set Single Lamp
1	30-11009	O Scale Cantilevered Bridge
1	30-11012	O Scale Operating Crossing Gate Signal Set
1	30-11014	O Scale Operating Crossing Flasher Set with Sound
1	30-11023	O Scale 3 Position Semaphore
1	30-11025	O Scale 1 Over 1 Signal
1	30-11028	Operating Water Tower
1	30-9031	Pennsylvania Switch Tower (Repainted for Santa Fe)
1	30-9043	Operating Coaling Tower
1	30-9044	Row House #1 Brown
1	30-9050	Passenger Station with Dual Platforms
1	30-9107	Operating Station Platform
1	30-9111	Operating Freight Platform
2	40-9014	Tunnel Portal (Single)

M.T.H. Digital Command System

Quantity	Item #	Description
1	40-4000	Z-4000 Transformer
1	50-1001	DCS Remote Control System – includes Handheld and Track Interface Unit (TIU)
1	50-1004	Accessory Interface Unit (AIU)
1	50-1007	TIU/TMCC 6' Connector Cable
3	50-1014	Layout Wiring Terminal Block

Sample Track Layout Plans Using RR-Track Layout Design Software

Layout 1

Size: 6' x 3'

Description: A basic layout that fits in a small space. It provides simple freight car switching opportunities to serve industries via the two sidings.

M.T.H. RealTrax Track Requirements:
(9) 40-1002 O-31 Curve
(10) 40-1001 10 Inch Straight
(2) 40-1005 O-31 Left-hand Switch
(2) 40-1018 3.5 Inch Straight
(2) 40-1024 Bumper
(1) 40-1017 4.25 in Straight

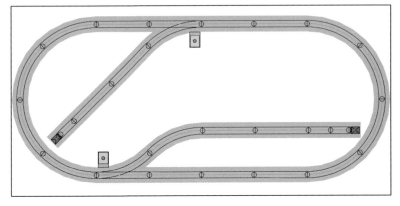

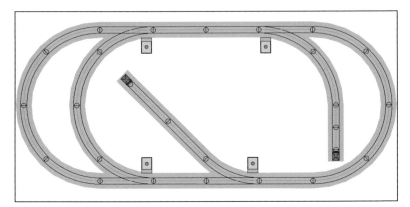

Layout 2

Size: 6' x 3'

Description: This variation of Layout 1 adds a pair of switches to form a double-ended siding on the left side. Combined with two sidings to serve industries, this layout will provide plenty of action when operating your trains.

M.T.H. RealTrax Track Requirements:
(11) 40-1002 O-31 Curve
(6) 40-1001 10 Inch Straight
(1) 40-1005 O-31 Left-hand Switch
(2) 40-1017 4.25 Inch Straight
(2) 40-1024 Bumper
(3) 40-1004 O-31 Right-hand Switch

Layout 3

Size: 8' x 3'

Description: Compact layout that includes a reversing loop in addition to a double-ended siding for operational variety. It also includes two long sidings allowing for multiple freight cars to serve industries.

M.T.H. RealTrax Track Requirements:
(11) 40-1002 O-31 Curve
(4) 40-1005 O-31 Left-hand Switch
(6) 40-1001 10 Inch Straight
(5) 40-1017 4.25 Inch Straight
(2) 40-1004 O-31 Right-hand Switch
(2) 40-1024 Bumper
(1) 40-1018 3.5 Inch Straight
(2) 40-1019 30 Inch Straight

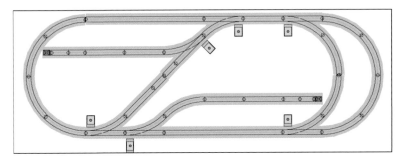

Layout 4

Size: 6' x 3'

Description: This expanded figure-eight track plan has five sidings to serve various industries. Your switch engine will certainly stay busy moving freight cars around on this layout.

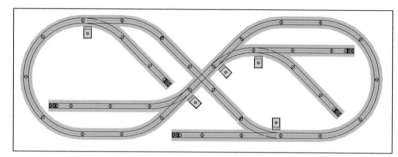

M.T.H. RealTrax Track Requirements:
- (11) 40-1002 O-31 Curve
- (1) 40-1006 90 Degree Cross
- (11) 40-1001 10 Inch Straight
- (5) 40-1004 O-31 Right-hand Switch
- (2) 40-1018 3.5 Inch Straight
- (5) 40-1024 Bumper
- (2) 40-1016 5.0 Inch Straight
- (1) 40-1012 5.5 Inch half Straight

Layout 5

Size: 8' x 4'

Description: This slightly larger layout will fit on a standard-sized piece of plywood while giving the operator many options. It includes a small yard, double-ended passing siding, and two sidings with a crossover for industries. A divider like the one used on the Santa Fe Raton Pass Railroad can easily be inserted in this layout plan.

M.T.H. RealTrax Track Requirements:
- (9) 40-1001 10 Inch Straight
- (11) 40-1002 O-31 Curve
- (8) 40-1012 5.5 Inch half Straight
- (1) 40-1007 45 Degree Cross
- (1) 40-1021 O-72 Left-hand Switch
- (2) 40-1020 O-72 Right-hand Switch
- (4) 40-1018 3.5 Inch Straight
- (5) 40-1016 5.0 Inch Straight
- (2) 40-1005 O-31 Left-hand Switch
- (2) 40-1017 4.25 Inch Straight
- (2) 40-1010 O-72 Curve
- (1) 40-1004 O-31 Right-hand Switch
- (2) 40-1019 30 Inch Straight
- (4) 40-1024 Bumper

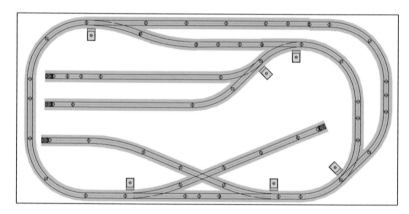

Layout 6

Size: 8' x 4'

Description: A large sweeping curve with plenty of sidings will provide for the servicing of multiple industries on this layout. Multiple radius track and switches give this layout a unique flavor while providing many operational possibilities.

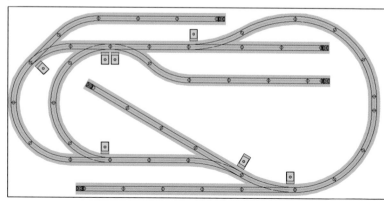

M.T.H. RealTrax Track Requirements:
- (7) 40-1002 O-31 Curve
- (18) 40-1001 10 Inch Straight
- (1) 40-1005 O-31 Left-hand Switch
- (3) 40-1004 O-31 Right-hand Switch
- (5) 40-1024 Bumper
- (2) 40-1055 O-54 Left-hand turnout
- (6) 40-1042 O-42 Curve
- (1) 40-1054 O-54 Curve
- (2) 40-1018 3.5 Inch Straight
- (1) 40-1056 O-54 Right-hand turnout

Layout 7

Size: 8' x 4'

Description: Busy is what the operator will be on this layout. It features a figure-eight design and combines it with a basic loop. The layout has several sidings for industries as well as a double-ended siding to store freight cars or serve as an interchange to another railroad.

M.T.H. RealTrax Track Requirements:
(10) 40-1002 O-31 Curve
(1) 40-1006 90 Degree Cross
(14) 40-1001 10 Inch Straight
(6) 40-1004 O-31 Right-hand Switch
(6) 40-1005 O-31 Left-hand Switch
(2) 40-1018 3.5 Inch Straight
(4) 40-1024 Bumper
(8) 40-1012 5.5 Inch Half Straight
(2) 40-1016 5.0 Inch Straight
(2) 40-1017 4.25 Inch Straight

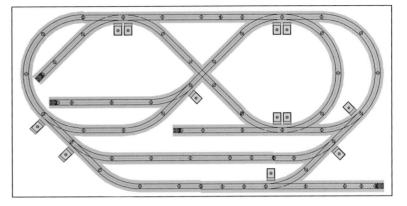

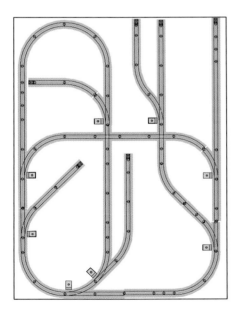

Layout 8

Size: 10' x 6'

Description: Dual 90 degree crossovers highlight this sprawling layout in which two loops are blended together with shared track. The layout also provides a small yard area where freight trains can depart and arrive allowing for plenty of switching action while passenger trains run on the main line.

M.T.H. RealTrax Track Requirements:
(18) 40-1001 10 Inch Straight
(14) 40-1002 O-31 Curve
(2) 40-1004 O-31 Right-hand Switch
(2) 40-1006 90 Degree Cross
(2) 40-1012 5.5 Inch Half Straight
(6) 40-1018 3.5 Inch Straight
(6) 40-1017 4.25 Inch Straight
(7) 40-1016 5.0 Inch Straight
(6) 40-1005 O-31 Left-hand Switch
(6) 40-1024 Bumper
(1) 40-1019 30 Inch Straight

Layout 9

Size: 12' x 8'

Description: This extended figure-eight track plan will fit nicely on two standard-sized sheets of plywood placed in an L configuration. It provides for a long mainline run with sweeping turns using O-42 curves and has several sidings for industries as well as a double-ended siding for challenging switching opportunities.

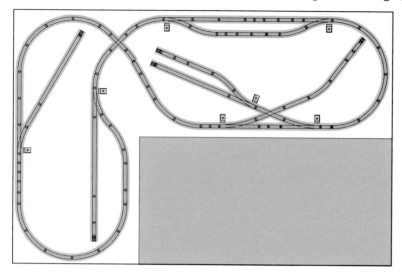

M.T.H. RealTrax Track Requirements:
(25) 40-1042 O-42 Curve
(6) 40-1045 O-42 Half Curve
(1) 40-1006 90 Degree Cross
(10) 40-1001 10 Inch Straight
(10) 40-1012 5.5 Inch Half Straight
(7) 40-1017 4.25 Inch Straight
(2) 40-1044 O-42 Left-hand Switch
(3) 40-1043 O-42 Right-hand Switch
(9) 40-1018 3.5 Inch Straight
(3) 40-1016 5.0 Inch Straight
(1) 40-1021 O-72 Left-hand Switch
(1) 40-1007 45 Degree Cross
(1) 40-1020 O-72 Right-hand Switch
(5) 40-1024 Bumper
(3) 40-1019 30 Inch Straight

Layout 10

Size: 12' x 8'

Description: Two railroads on one layout. If you have two favorite railroads you like to operate (such as New York Central and Pennsylvania), then this track plan is for you. Plenty of action with various sidings on each are connected via an interchange track that uses a crossover. This allows for the actual exchange of freight cars between the two railroads in which you can simulate as mentioned in the Dispatcher Game chapter.

M.T.H. RealTrax Track Requirements:
(25) 40-1042 O-42 Curve
(18) 40-1001 10 Inch Straight
(4) 40-1043 O-42 Right-hand Switch
(1) 40-1007 45 Degree Cross
(3) 40-1016 5.0 in Straight
(2) 40-1010 O-72 Curve
(1) 40-1057 O-54 Half Curve
(7) 40-1012 5.5 Inch Half Straight
(13) 40-1018 3.5 Inch Straight
(1) 40-1055 O-54 Left-hand Switch
(6) 40-1017 4.25 in Straight
(4) 40-1044 O-42 Left-hand Switch
(5) 40-1024 Bumper
(1) 40-1045 O-42 Half Curve
(9) 40-1002 O-31 Curve
(2) 40-1005 O-31 Left-hand Switch

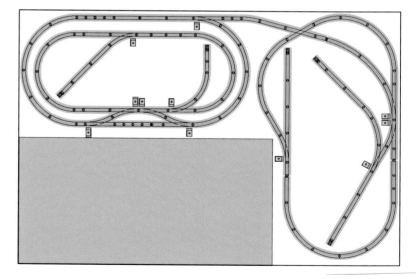

APPENDIX 5

Scenery Application Quick Reference Tip Sheet

Tip	Reason
Work on one section at a time	Working on small areas at a time allows you see results as you go along. It also allows you to mix colors and other items such as Lightweight Hydrocal in small batches for application on the layout.
Observe the real thing	To create a mountain, try to observe a real mountain. If case you can't, look in books or watch videos to see what a real mountain looks like – especially for the area or region you are modeling.
Work from light to dark and small to big	When applying coloring or adding vegetation, start light or small and work your way up. It is much easier to add more color or vegetation than it is to take it off.
Stand back and look	When applying coloring or vegetation, it is easy to get up too close. Be sure to stand back every few minutes and view it from farther away. You see it looks differently from a distance, which is how other people will observe it.
Avoid mono-color	With the exception of some lawns in your neighborhood, rarely will you find any scenery that is uniform in color. To avoid this, lightly sprinkle Fine Turf in a different color such as Burnt Grass onto trees, grass, and bushes.
Bigger to smaller up the mountain	When applying bushes and trees to a mountain, it is best to start with the larger ones down around the bottom. As you work your way up the mountain, use smaller and smaller items. This will help create an illusion (referred to as Forced Perspective) of greater distance and make the mountains seem larger than it is to the person observing it.

Over the last decade, the number of O gauge model railroad clubs has grown substantially. These types of layouts these clubs share are usually large, and jointly owned by members. In the operation of such layouts, there is one particular feature of DCS called Proto-Dispatch that can be utilized to help in club layout operation. Though this feature was designed to allow operators to make their own station announcements via a ProtoSound 2.0 equipped engine through the microphone built into the DCS Remote, Proto-Dispatch can also be used to communicate with club members to ensure that their MTH Electric Trains run smoothly.

A sample Train List similar to one used in *The Dispatcher Game* (see Chapter 10) for the model railroad club is shown below. All of the members involved in the illustration have their own DCS Remote and are running their ProtoSound 2.0 equipped locomotives. The club member designated as the dispatcher will not operate a train, but rather use the Proto-Dispatch feature by speaking instructions for the specific club member's train into the microphone built into the DCS Remote. The resulting instructions will emanate from the club member's locomotive engine telling him to pull his train onto a siding or slow down to a certain speed. To stay on top of the action, the dispatcher must be positioned where he can see most of the train layout.

Using the DCS Remote in this manner not only gives operators a tool to control their trains, but it also doubles as a communication device as well.

TOOG Model Railroad Club   **Date: 4/27/2002**

Dispatcher: Tony L.

E Clockwise
W Counter-clockwise

Train List

Class	Operator	Motive Power	Dir	Type
Second	Tom G.	UP 844 4-8-4	E	Reefers
First	Rob A. *Super Chief*	ATSF F-3 16	W	Passenger
Third	Randy T.	BNSF Dash-9 4635	W	Hoppers - Grain
First	Steve G. *Phoebe Snow*	DL&W F-3 801	E	Passenger
First	Frank R.	NH F-3 2242 Caboose C-701	W	Automobile Flats
First	Gary F. *20th Century Limited*	NYC 5445 4-6-4	W	Passenger
Second	Roy T.	WP 483 4-8-4	W	Mixed Freight
First	Rich G. *The Chief*	ATSF 3460 4-6-4	E	Passenger
Second	Terry S.	UP 2535 2-8-2 Caboose 25724	W	Reefers
Second	Cam M.	ON 2103 SD70M Caboose 128	E	Hoppers - Grain
First	Steve M.	UP M32 Doodlebug	W	Passenger
Second	Tom D.	ATSF 5012 2-10-4 Caboose 1579	E	Mixed Freight
First	Mark A. *Florida Special*	FEC E-6a 1004	E	Passenger

Crossing Gate Article on Building the RailTown Milling Co.

My father-in-law, Ted Cheatham, followed the Model Shop article from the February 2001 issues of the Crossing Gate Newsletter (shown below) to create the Trinity Transport Company for the Santa Fe Raton Pass Railroad. One of the benefits of the M.T.H. Model Railroader's Club is receiving the Crossing Gate Newsletter.

the MODEL SHOP

BUILDING YOUR OWN LOADING DOCK

For this month's "Model Shop," Ted makes a loading dock from two of M.T.H.'s country houses. This project is perfect for a working industrial layout, especially one where you can arrange to have tracks on one side of the building and a truck bay on the other. The frame windows and "wood" siding make this loading dock especially appropriate for a small town layout set in the twentieth century.

Ted starts by removing all the windows, doors, awnings, and stone foundations from the houses and cutting the small wing off one of the houses. He then determines which walls will butt together and cuts off the roof overhangs on those sides of the main houses and small wings even with the walls. The next step is to join the two main sections together, end to end, and to join the lone addition to the end of the

new building, so that the two main wings are side-by-side, and the two smaller wings are side-by-side, attached to one end of the main wings. The small wing has two upper mounts that have to be cut off before it will sit flush with the adjacent wall. Next Ted puts glue in the roof seams, then fills them with putty to make them smooth.

Ted uses .060 styrene to make a new, more industrial-looking foundation for the building. He makes it 20 mm. high all the way around the building and additions, to make them the right height for the delivery trailers.

To make the bay doors, Ted creates a template 35 mm. wide and 40 mm. high. He spaces the door openings evenly along the front and back of

the small wing and cuts out holes for the doors. The doors themselves are made of corrugated plastic sheet glued to the inside of the wall, covering the bays.

The loading dock is made of .060 styrene sheet 20 mm. high to match the height of the foundation and with a platform 31mm. deep for the truck dock and 22mm. deep for the train dock. Ted makes the loading dock roof out of the narrow part of the front porch awning cut away from the house in step one.

At this point, all the trim needs to be put on the loading dock. Ted replaces the windows and doors, builds the steps from .060 styrene sheet, and, for a detailed touch, uses rubber strips to make the bumpers on the truck side of the dock. The supports for the dock roof are made of .025 brass rod, as are the step railings. The roof sign is 11" x 1½". ∎

Difficulty Rating (on a scale of 1-5): 3

Time to Complete: 3 days

Bibliography

Videos:

Santa Fe Warbonnets through Raton Pass, "Machines of Iron" Series, Produced by Spinnaker Home Video, Program copyright 1997 Spinnaker Presentations

Raton Pass: King Coal, The Chief, and the "BALJ", Produced by Pentrex, Pasadena, CA, Copyright Pentrex 1994.

Books:

Model Railroader's Handbook: An Introduction and How-To Guide from RailKing and M.T.H. Electric Trains, by M.T.H. Electric Trains. Written by Andrew Arvesen, Edited by Kristin Bailey, Copyright 2001 by M.T.H. Electric Trains, Columbia, Maryland.

Drury, George H., *The Golden Years of Railroading: Santa Fe in the Mountains – Three Passes of the West: Raton, Cajon, and Tehachapi*, Copyright 1995 by Kalmbach Publishing Co., Waukesha, Wisconsin

Harper, Jared V., *Santa Fe's Raton Pass*, Copyright 1983 by Jared V. Harper, published by Kachina Press, 1983, Dallas, TX

Berkman, Pamela, *The History of the Atchison, Topeka & Santa Fe*, Copyright 1988 Brompton Books Corp., published 1995 by SMITHMARK Publishers Inc., New York, New York.

Glischinski, Steve, *Railroad Color History, Santa Fe Railway*, Copyright 1997 Andover Junction Publications, published 1997 by Motorbooks International Publishers & Wholesalers, Osceola, WI

Santa Fe in the Intermountain West: Colorado Rail Annual No. 23, A Journal of Railroad History in the Rocky Mountain West, Editors: Kenton Forrest, Richard Cooley & Charles Albi; Copyright 1998 by the Colorado Railroad Historical Foundation, Inc., published and distributed by Colorado Railroad Museum, Golden, CO

M.T.H. Electric Trains, *A Toy Train Story: The Remarkable History of M.T.H. Electric Trains*, Copyright 2000 by M.T.H. Electric Trains, Columbia, Maryland

Greenberg's Guide to M.T.H. Electric Trains, First Edition, Copyright 2000 Kalmbach Publishing Co., published by Kalmbach Publishing Co., Waukesha, WI

Internet:

http://www.gatewaynmra.org/designops.htm

About the Author

Rob Adelman grew up in a suburb of Chicago and was first introduced the hobby of model railroading at the age of five years old when he received his first set of toy trains at Christmas. He has been an avid participant in the hobby ever since. A key turning point in his interest came during 1994 when Rob was introduced to M.T.H. Electric Trains. He had become disenchanted with other manufacturer's high prices and low quality, which almost caused Rob to leave the hobby. He found M.T.H. Electric Trains to be the perfect fit for his avid interest in O gauge trains due to their variety, quality, and value. Ever since that time he has been a strong supporter, enthusiastic fan, and purchaser of M.T.H. Electric Trains.

Rob's other interests include spending time with family, playing hockey (and sports in general), Rush Limbaugh, eating New Mexico Green Chile, and being an active member of his church. Rob, his wife Amie, daughter Elizabeth, and their Shetland Sheepdogs—Rusty and Daisy, reside in a suburb of Dallas, Texas.

Rob can be reached via email at radelman@aol.com